About the Authors

Bruce Joyce directs Booksend Laboratories, based in Pauma Valley, California. His work is divided between extensive school renewal programs in school districts and foreign countries and research on teaching, curriculum, staff development, and school renewal. His recent books include *Models of Teaching*, 5th edition; *Learning Experiences in School Renewal*, coedited with Emily Calhoun; *The Self-Renewing School*, coauthored with Emily Calhoun and Jim Wolf; and *Student Achievement Through Staff Development*, coauthored with Beverly Showers. He can be reached at P.O. Box 175, Pauma Valley, CA 92061. Telephone and Fax: 619-742-3190.

Emily Calhoun directs The Phoenix Alliance, based in St. Simons Island, Georgia. A specialist in language arts and action research, she divides her time between extensive school renewal programs and research on teaching and action research. She is author of *How to Use Action Research in the Self-Renewing School* and collaborated in the development of the ASCD video-based, staff development program *Action Research: Inquiry, Reflection, and Decision Making*. She can be reached at 624 Demere Way, St. Simons Island, GA 31522. Telephone and Fax: 912-638-0685.

Creating Learning Experiences: The Role of Instructional Theory and Research

Creating Learning Experiences

The Role of
Instructional Theory
and Research

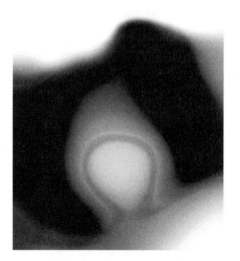

Bruce R. Joyce and Emily F. Calhoun

Association for Supervision and Curriculum Development
Alexandria, Virginia

Association for Supervision and Curriculum Development
1250 N. Pitt Street • Alexandria, Virginia 22314-1453
Telephone: 1-800-933-2723 or 703-549-9110 • Fax: 703-299-8631

Gene R. Carter, *Executive Director*
Michelle Terry, *Assistant Executive Director, Program Development*
Ronald S. Brandt, *Assistant Executive Director*
Nancy Modrak, *Managing Editor, ASCD Books*
Margaret A. Oosterman, *Associate Editor*
Beth Kabele, *Project Assistant*
Gary Bloom, *Manager, Design and Production Services*
Karen Monaco, *Designer*
Tracey A. Smith, *Production Coordinator*
Dina Murray, *Production Assistant*
Valerie Sprague, *Desktop Publisher*

Printed in the United States of America.

ASCD Stock No. 196229
Member $11.95
Nonmember $13.95
s10/96

Library of Congress Cataloging-in-Publication Data

Joyce, Bruce R.
    Creating learning experiences : the role of instructional theory
and research / Bruce R. Joyce, Emily F. Calhoun.
        p.   cm.
    Includes bibliographical references.
    ISBN 0-87120-272-7
    1. Learning.   2. Education—Research.   3. Education—Experimental
methods.   4. Teaching.   I. Calhoun, Emily.   II. Title.
LB1026.J69   1996
371.39–dc20   96-35606
                                                                  CIP

00 99 98 97 96   5 4 3 2 1

Foreword

When I was a student in elementary and secondary school, there was basically one model of teaching, sometimes called lecture recitation. Teachers stood at the front of the class, explained concepts and skills, assigned seat work, and checked the seat work. They asked many questions, but otherwise, we were expected to be passive listeners or quiet workers most of the time. Some teachers did a good job with this kind of instruction, and some students did learn from it. But day in, day out, 180 days a year, year after year, the lecture recitation got, let's say, a little tired. So did we. The best students were usually bored, and our less academically inclined classmates simply dropped out mentally and emotionally long before they dropped out physically.

The lecture recitation model is still with us, of course, and more than a few students still find school less than scintillating. Today, however, there is vastly more variety in teaching methods than 20 years ago. Walk through any school anywhere and you're likely to see at least some teachers implementing cooperative learning or project-based learning, mnemonics or advance organizers, inquiry or discovery. Even when they do use lecture recitation methods, they often incorporate strategies from such models as Madeline Hunter's "mastery teaching" or mastery learning.

At least part of the credit for the increasing variety of instructional models that teachers use at all levels must go to Bruce Joyce and his colleagues. For more than a quarter century, Joyce has been describing the rich array of alternatives that should be in every teacher's repertoire and synthesizing the research on these models. *Creating Learning Experiences* continues this tradition, describing "families" of instructional models in clear, accessible language, with many examples to help readers place theory into classroom context. I hope this book will further contribute to helping teachers use more diverse and research-based strategies to meet the needs of their students.

—ROBERT SLAVIN

Scenarios

Mr. Hendricks's 4th grade students enter their classroom after lunch to find an array of glasses, bottles, bells, wooden boxes of different sizes—some with holes—tuning forks, xylophones, and small wooden flutes. These objects are spread about the room, and the students spend a few minutes playing with them, creating a most horrendous sound. Mr. Hendricks watches and listens.

After a few minutes, the students begin to settle down, and one of them asks, "What's going on here, Mr. Hendricks? It looks like you've turned the place into an orchestra."

"Well, in a way," he smiles. "Actually, for the next few weeks, this is going to be our sound laboratory." He moves across the room, picks up a box, and plucks one of the wires fastened to it. Simultaneously, he uses a spoon to strike a soft drink bottle on the desk next to him. "Do you notice anything about these sounds?" he asks, and repeats his plucking and striking.

"Hey," says Joan, "they sound the same, but different."

"Do it again, please," suggests Mike, and Mr. Hendricks obliges. Soon all the students have noticed that the sound is at the same pitch or level.

"Your job," explains Mr. Hendricks, "is to find out what makes sound vary and to describe that variation. Given the limitations of the devices we have in this room, I want you to organize yourselves to conduct some experiments and present me with sets of principles that you think describe the variations. When you're finished, you should be able to describe how you would design an instrument with certain capabilities. I'll tell you what I want the instrument to be able to do, and you can tell me how to make it. Then we'll begin to test your ideas. Now, I think we ought to organize ourselves into groups and decide how we're going to go about this. Does anybody have any ideas?"

"Well," Sally ventures, "I've noticed that the things are made out of five different kinds of materials. Maybe we can get into five groups and each group can experiment with those for a while. Then we share what we've learned and trade around and check out the thinking of the other groups. After that, we can decide what to do next."

Someone joins in with another suggestion, and the class spends the next half hour planning how the study will begin.

SCENARIO II

Five-year-old Brendan sits in a circle with the other children in Omega School's primary computer center. In front of each student is a Galaxy Pentium computer, networked to the others, including those at the teachers' workstation. The teachers' displays are projected to large screens on opposite sides of the room. All monitors show the WordPerfect 6.1 screen blank and ready to receive words. A model of the Omega School neighborhood is in the middle of the circle. The children used construction paper to build the houses and stores, which sit on a map painted on butcher paper.

The teacher, Jeanie Jones, opens a discussion of the model by talking about the walks students have taken, things they have observed, and decisions about what was included in their model of the neighborhood. Then she says, "Now, let's talk about what we've learned and write down some of those things." Brendan raises his hand, but Ms. Jones calls on Sally.

"I think we found that parts of the town have houses, and other parts have stores," Sally says.

"Let me type that in for you," says Ms. Jones, and she does, using a large font. The children watch as the words appear on their screens. Then, Ms. Jones highlights the first word and continues to highlight the next words as the children repeat the words. She asks them to save the sentence on their own floppy disks under the file name "Our Town." The children have saved files before, but it is a few minutes before the task is accomplished, with help from each other, Ms. Jones, and the aide Mrs. Simons.

Another student has an idea. "We found that we have three doctors, four dentists, and one pet hospital." Ms. Jones types in the sentence, and the students read it together as she highlights the words. She asks them to read both sentences and save them under the same file name on their disks. Now, she asks that they read the sentences to themselves, highlighting the words as she has done.

The process continues. Two more sentences are added, read, and saved. The students read the four sentences together:

"I think we found that parts of the town have houses, and other parts have stores."

"We found that we have three doctors, four dentists, and one pet hospital."

"Some of us live close enough to the school to walk, but the others have to take the bus."

"The parks are where the houses are, not where the stores are."

Ms. Jones announces that they will stop at this point. She asks the students to print out their files and cut the words apart. They collect their piles of words in envelopes and take them, with their disks, back to their individual work areas. She says they will take a little recess and then come back and sort the words into groups according to how the words begin. By this time, Brendan is bursting, and she recognizes him.

He says, "Doctor and dentist start with the same letter, and they sound the same at the beginning."

Ms. Jones smiles and says, "That's right, Brendan, and that's exactly the kind of thing I want you to notice when you sort the words. We're studying our town, our computers, and learning to read, all at the same time."

SCENARIO III

Mary Hilltepper opens the year in her 10th grade English class by presenting the students with 12 poems that she has selected from a set of 100 poems, representing the works of prominent contemporary poets. After organizing the students into pairs, she asks them to read the poems, then classify them by structure, style, and theme. As the pairs classify the poems, she asks that they prepare to report their categories to the other pairs so that the partnerships can compare classifications. Working together, the class accumulates a list of ways they have discriminated structure, style, and theme. Ms. Hilltepper presents the student pairs with another dozen poems, which they examine, fitting them into the existing categories and expanding the categories as necessary. This process is repeated over the next few days until all students are familiar with four dozen poems. She then gives them several other tasks. One is to decide how particular themes are handled by style and structure and vice versa (i.e., if style and structure are correlated with each other and with themes). Another task is to build hypotheses about whether some groups of poems were written by particular authors, based upon distinctive combinations of style, structure, and theme.

After this activity, she hands out the anthologies and books of critical analysis that are the course textbooks, asking students to test their hypotheses about authorship and to find out if the authors of the poems employ the same categories the students have been developing.

Theme

Learning experiences are composed of content, process, and social climate. As educators, we strive to create for and with our children opportunities to explore and build important areas of knowledge, to develop powerful tools for learning, and to live in humanizing social conditions.

From our toolbox, we use models of teaching (actually, models for learning), which simultaneously define the nature of the content, learning strategies, and social interaction that will become part of our students. Depending on the models we select, content is conceptual or particular, process is constructive inquiry or passive reception, and the social climate is expansive or restrictive. Our choices depend on our teaching repertoire and our efforts to expand it by developing new models and studying those developed by others.

Our purpose in writing this book is to introduce readers to some of the teaching models that have been developed, polished, and studied during the modern era of educational research. We hope that teachers, teaching centers, school districts, and developers of curriculums and instructional materials will study these models and discover modes of teaching that have great power for learners. School faculties can use them to select foci for staff development, curriculum implementation, and action research. When well implemented, some of these models both accelerate rates of learning, sometimes several times, and bring within the reach of students types of conceptual control and modes of inquiry that have been difficult to generate through many of the most common teaching methods.

Interestingly, the most powerful models of teaching adapt easily to a wide spectrum of curriculum areas and types of learners. They work when teaching phonics and physics. They help the gifted and the most at risk. They do not tolerate socioeconomic or gender differences as inhibitors of learning but, instead, capitalize on those differences. Their effects are enhanced by variety in cultural and linguistic background.

Each model is an inquiry into teaching and learning; such inquiry is the basis for much of a model's strength. Rather than a formula to follow slavishly, each model brings us into the study of how our students learn and makes us reflective action researchers in our classrooms, reshaping environments for learning and selecting new experiences for our students.

We are grateful to the great teacher-researchers who gave us this rich professional heritage. In an attempt to solve problems of teaching, they exercised their splendid imaginations and followed their ideas with a tenacious pursuit of knowledge.

—BRUCE JOYCE AND EMILY CALHOUN

An Inquiry into Teaching and Learning

Last September, 100 years ago, I thought teaching was one job with a few variations. I had an image of the one kind of teaching I could do well, with the one kind of student I could see myself teaching well. It turned out that it is 20 jobs to do with 20 different personalities.

—A BEGINNING TEACHER TO BRUCE JOYCE
DECEMBER 1995

Thinking about the roles that make up teaching can make you dizzy. Just for starters, consider helping students grow in understanding and knowledge, self-awareness, moral development, and ability to relate to others.

Simultaneously, we are counselors, facilitators, instructional managers, curriculum designers, academic instructors, evaluators of instruction, and reluctantly, disciplinarians. To the best of our ability, we modulate across roles in response to individual and group needs, selecting and creating learning experiences for our students.

Creating these learning experiences requires a large repertoire of teaching strategies, so we have another built-in role—learning more ways of teaching so that we can select the best possible learning experi-

1

ences for each purpose and group of students and become increasingly skillful in the use of these strategies.

Consider these four teachers at work on the first day of school.

SCENARIO I: 1ST GRADE

In one 1st grade class, the children are gathered around a table with a candle and jar on it. The teacher, Jackie Wiseman, lights the candle, and after it has burned brightly for a minute or two, places the jar carefully over the candle. The candle grows dim, flickers, and goes out. Then she produces another candle and a larger jar and repeats the exercise. The candle goes out, but more slowly. Ms. Wiseman produces two more candles and jars of different sizes, and the children light the candles, place the jars over them, and the flames slowly go out.

"Now, we're going to develop some ideas about what has just happened," Ms. Wiseman says. "I want you to ask me questions about those candles and jars and what you just observed."

The students begin. She gently helps them rephrase their questions or plan experiments. One student asks, "Would the candles burn longer with an even bigger jar?"

Ms. Wiseman responds, "How might we find out?" Periodically, she asks them to tell her what they know and the questions they have, and she writes what they say on newsprint paper. Their own words will be the content of their first study of reading.

SCENARIO II: 1ST GRADE

Next door, the children are seated in pairs. A pile of small objects and a magnet are in front of each pair. Their teacher, John Fisher, smiles at them and explains that the U-shaped object is called a magnet.

"We're going to find out something about this thing we call a magnet," he says. "We'll begin by finding out what it does when it's held close to different things. So, I want you to explore with your magnet. Find out what happens when you bring it close to or touch the objects in front of you. And sort the other objects according to what happens." Like Jackie Wiseman, John Fisher will take notes on the categories the students form and use those to begin their study of written vocabulary.

COMMENTARY ON SCENARIOS I AND II

Jackie Wiseman began her year with the model of teaching we call *inquiry training*. The model starts with having students encounter what is, to them, a puzzling situation. By asking questions and conducting experiments, they build and test ideas. Jackie studies their inquiry and plans the next series of activities to build a community that can work together to explore their world.

John Fisher began with the model we call *inductive thinking*. That model first presents students with information or asks them to collect information and engage in classifying. As the students develop categories, in this case, the response of objects to what the kids will eventually learn to call a magnetic field, they build hypotheses to test. John studies how they think and what they see and don't see and helps them learn to attack other areas as a community of inductive thinkers.

SCENARIO III: 10TH GRADE

Mariam True's 10th grade social studies class begins with a videotape taken in a California courtroom. Litigation is in progress over whether a mother can prevent a father and their 12-year-old son from having time together. The parents are divorced and have joint custody of their son, who lives with the mother.

The tape presents the opening arguments in the case. Ms. True asks the students to generate individually the issues as they see them and questions requiring further information. She then asks them to share the issues and questions and requests that each student accumulate the information under the headings "issues" and "questions." The students find that they need to develop another category, "positions and values," because many of the students articulated positions during the sharing exercise.

The inquiry continues by watching more tape segments and analyzing several abstracts of similar cases that Ms. True has collected. One such case is their first homework assignment. Gradually, through the week, Ms. True leads the students to develop sets of policy statements and identify the values that underlie the possible policies. As the inquiry proceeds, she will study how well the students can clarify facts, distinguish value positions from one another, and discuss differences between seemingly opposing values and policy positions. She, too, is beginning the development of a learning inquiry and is an inquirer into her students and their learning.

SCENARIO IV: 10TH GRADE

Now let's move to Shirley Mills's English course, which opens with a scene from the film *The Milagra Beanfield War*. The students share their reactions to the setting, actions, and characters introduced in the scene, expressing a variety of different views. When they want to defend their interpretations or argue against the ideas of others, Ms. Mills announces that for now, she wants to preserve their differences so that they can inquire into them. She next passes out copies of the novel *The Milagra Beanfield War* by John Nichols and asks them to begin reading it. During the week, she will lead them to develop an inquiry into the social issues that the book and film present and to compare the film with the book to study the devices the author and film makers use. Ms. Mills will watch closely to determine what issues and devices they see and don't see as she builds her community of learners.

COMMENTARY ON SCENARIOS III AND IV

Mariam True opened her class with the *jurisprudential inquiry* model of teaching, which is designed to lead students in the study of public policy issues and their own values.

Shirley Mills introduced her students to the *group investigation* model, a powerful cooperative learning model she has used to design her course. The model begins with a confrontation with information that leads to an area of inquiry. The students inquire into their perceptual worlds, including similarities and differences in perception as the inquiries proceed.

Keeping these four teachers and classes in mind, let's return to the discussion of our work. As we teach, we try to find out the learning that has occurred and the readiness for new learning. But teachers cannot crawl inside students' heads and look around—we have to infer what is inside from what we can see and hear. Making educated guesses is part of our profession, as we continually try to construct in *our* minds the pictures of what our students are experiencing.

The never-ending cycles of arranging environments, providing tasks, and building pictures of students' minds determine the character of teaching. Inquiry into mind and environment never completes itself—one episode runs into another.

The inquiry process that guides the creation of learning experiences is the same at all levels, from primary through graduate school. An algebra teacher and a physics professor arrange environments, provide tasks, and try to learn what is going on in their students' minds, just as the teacher who first introduces her students to reading and writing.

The problem of designing learning experiences is central to the study of teaching. Searching for solutions guides the research that has spawned the models we draw on. These models are the products of teacher-researchers who have beaten a path for us and given us a head start in our inquiries. Throughout the inquiry process, we operate on three theses to guide us in developing such products:

• *Teachers have an extensive array of alternative approaches to use in teaching.* Many approaches are practical and can be implemented in classrooms and schools where teachers have the will and skill. These teaching models are sufficiently different from one another to increase the probability that different outcomes will result when they are used (see Joyce and Weil 1996).

• *Methods make a difference in what is learned as well as how it is learned.* The difference is probabilistic: Particular methods boost certain outcomes and diminish others, but rarely do they guarantee some while obliterating the rest.

• *Students are a powerful part of the learning experience being created, and they react differently to any given teaching method.* A combination of personality, aptitudes, interpersonal skills, and previous achievement contributes to configurations of learning styles, so that no two people react exactly the same way to any one model of teaching.

A primary task of teachers and faculties is to equip themselves with a variety of teaching models that they can use for different purposes, adapt for different learners, and combine artfully to create classrooms and learning communities of variety and depth. This work requires clarity about what models exist, what the models can accomplish, and how different students react to them.

Using a variety of models comfortably and effectively requires study and practice (see Chapter 7), but by concentrating on one or two at a time, we can easily expand our repertoires. One key to improving our skills is to use the models as tools of inquiry. A second key is to understand that the models of teaching are really *models of learning*. As we help students acquire information, ideas, skills, values, ways of thinking, and means of expressing themselves, we are also teaching them how to learn. In fact, *the most important long-term outcome of instruction may be students' increased capabilities to learn more easily and effectively in the future, both because of the knowledge and skill they have acquired and because they have mastered learning processes.*

In this book, we introduce some of these models of teaching, discuss their underlying theories, examine the research that has tested them, and provide scenarios that illustrate their uses. Once mastered, they become tools of our craft that help us better fulfill our multiple responsibilities as we create learning experiences.

The Families of
Teaching Models

2

*At first, when people create or find a new model of teaching
that works for some purpose, they're so thrilled they try to use
it for everything. Our job is to provide some order—finding
out what each model can do and building categories to help
folks find the tools they need.*

—BRUCE JOYCE
AGAIN AND AGAIN IN STAFF MEETINGS FROM 1965 TO THE PRESENT

My colleagues and I have been searching for promising approaches to
teaching since the late 1950s. The hunt has many facets. We visit
schools (30 last year) and classrooms (200 last year); interview teachers;
study research on teaching and learning; and observe people in teaching roles outside schools, such as therapists and trainers in industrial,
military, and athletic settings.

We found models of teaching in abundance. These models range
from simple procedures that students can easily respond to, to complex
strategies that students gradually acquire through patient and skillful
instruction. Some models aim at specific objectives; others have a
broader usefulness. Some are quite formal; others are casual and emer-
gent. All address a variety of objectives in the personal, social, and

7

academic domains and encompass our major responsibilities as teachers.

From the late 1950s until the mid-1970s, research sponsored by foundations, the federal government, and school districts refined long-standing teaching models and developed new ones to a degree not seen before or since. Some research concentrated on specific curriculum areas, particularly language arts, social studies, science, and mathematics. During the same period, research on effective teachers and schools shed light on teacher practices. Over the last 20 years, research on mnemonics and cooperative learning has redeveloped and refined models in those areas, and research on training has clarified how people acquire skills and apply (transfer) them to solve problems. Recent work on how students construct knowledge is enriching the models, as is research on how students develop the "metacognitions" that enable them to consciously improve their strategies for learning. Individual teachers and school faculties can use these models of teaching as instructional strategies and guides when planning lessons, units, courses, and curriculums and when designing classroom activities and instructional materials.

To bring order into the study of the growing storehouse of models, we grouped them into four families: information-processing, social, personal, and behavioral systems. Each family is characterized by the types of learning its models promote and its orientation toward people and how people learn.

The models we selected for each family are based on practicability criteria; that is, the models have considerable utility in instructional settings. Thus, they have long histories of practice behind them: Experience has refined them so that they can be used comfortably and efficiently in classrooms and other educational settings. They are adaptable: They can be adjusted to the learning styles of students and to the requirements of subject matter. They have lifetime utility, becoming learning tools for life: Most are useful across the elementary and secondary grades, as well as at the university level. And finally, evidence shows that they work in enhancing students' ability to learn: All are backed by formal research that tests their theories and abilities to effect learning.

THE INFORMATION-PROCESSING FAMILY

Information-processing models emphasize ways of enhancing a human being's drive to make sense of the world by acquiring and organizing data, sensing problems and generating solutions to them, and developing concepts and language for conveying the solutions. Some of the models provide the learner with information and concepts (e.g., concept attainment); some emphasize concept formation and hypothesis testing (e.g., inductive thinking); and others generate creative thinking (e.g., synectics). A few are designed to enhance general intellectual ability. Many information-processing models are useful for studying the self and society, and thus for achieving the personal and social goals of education. The References and Bibliography sections of the book include the primary works of the developers.

Information-processing models, as the name implies, are to help students learn to process information. In addition, while the students are collecting and operating on information, they acquire knowledge, usually in the form of observations or data from books and other sources. Higher-order knowledge is then constructed, beginning with simple classifications and ranging up the scale to the structures of knowledge in academic fields and finally to theoretical knowledge, including the alternative ways that theories are developed. For example, processing that begins with discriminating the letter *A* from the letter *B* can eventually be elaborated into the linguistic theories that attempt to explain how language learning reflects and enhances cognitive processes and whether there are cognitive differences between cultures.

All the information-processing models are designed to help students develop a conscious awareness of strategies for learning and use those strategies to inquire into and reflect upon their world. Thus, these models have much in common, which is why they are grouped together. They all share the purpose of developing inquiring learners. Their structures and purposes, however, are distinctive through what they emphasize–the tools for learning and the aspects of content that they enable learners to explore. Figure 2.1 (see p. 10) lists the information processing models, identifies their developers, and briefly explores the kinds of learning they emphasize.

FIGURE 2.1	Information-Processing Models	
MODEL	**DEVELOPER (Redeveloper)**	**PURPOSE**
Inductive Thinking (Classification)	Hilda Taba (Bruce Joyce)	Learning how to classify is fundamental; consequently, students learn information and concepts through the activity of classifying. They also learn how to build conceptual understanding of content areas and how to build and test hypotheses based on classifications. Inductive thinking is a generic model, partly because classification is believed to be the basic higher-order thinking skill and further, because the model is applicable to knowledge from phonics to physics.
Concept Attainment	Jerome Bruner Fred Lighthall (Bruce Joyce)	Directly helps students learn specific concepts and study strategies for attaining them. Extensions lead students in the same direction as the inductive thinking model, gaining control over areas of content, learning to build hypotheses, and studying thinking.
Scientific Inquiry	Joseph Schwab and many others	Brings students into the community of academic inquirers. Helps them learn the modes of inquiry of the disciplines and in the process learn the knowledge base and major concepts of the disciplines. Develops conceptual thinking, hypothetical reasoning, and critical capacity.
Inquiry Training	Richard Suchman (Howard Jones)	A program to "train" students to reason causally. Thus, learning to collect data, build concepts, and develop and test hypotheses are central to its purposes.

MODEL	DEVELOPER (Redeveloper)	PURPOSE

FIGURE 2.1   Information-Processing Models (continued)

MODEL	DEVELOPER (Redeveloper)	PURPOSE
Cognitive Growth	Jean Piaget Irving Sigel Constance Kamii Edmund Sullivan	Generating increased general intellectual growth is the major objective. In advanced applications, this model helps students understand the nature of cognitive growth and how they can facilitate their own development.
Advance Organizer	David Ausubel (many others)	Increases ability to absorb information and organize it, especially when learning from lectures and readings.
Mnemonics	Michael Pressley Joel Levin (and associated scholars)	Helps students develop strategies for acquiring information, concepts, and complex structures of concepts (e.g., the Table of Chemical Elements). Leads students toward metacognitive control—the conscious understanding of learning strategies and when and how to use them.
Synectics	Bill Gordon	Leads students to inquire into metaphoric thinking through the use of analogies.

THE SOCIAL FAMILY: BUILDING A LEARNING COMMUNITY

When we work together, we generate collective energy called synergy. The social models of teaching are constructed to take advantage of this phenomenon by building learning communities (see Figure 2.2 on pp. 13–14). Essentially, classroom management involves developing cooperative relationships in a classroom. Creating a positive school culture is a process of developing integrative and productive ways of interacting and norms that support vigorous learning activity.

Social models are alike in that they share the objectives of increasing social skill and synergy and ultimately imbuing students with social commitment and the tools to participate in the highest forms of democratic process. All the models encourage respect for others and the development of strong personal values. All help students learn to construct knowledge through collective inquiry. The social models, however, are distinguished from each other in the aspects of social interaction they foster and in the breadth of social goals they address. Sometimes it is not recognized that all these models help students learn information, concepts, and advanced academic skills. Their genre, however, is characterized by the overriding importance of the social goals and processes for achieving them.

THE PERSONAL FAMILY

Ultimately, human reality resides in our individual consciousnesses. We develop unique personalities and see the world from perspectives that are the products of our particular experiences and positions. Common understandings result from the negotiation of individuals who must live and work and create families and communities together.

The personal models of learning begin from the perspective of an individual's selfhood (see Figure 2.3 on p. 15). They attempt to shape education so that we can understand ourselves better; take responsibility for our education; and learn to reach beyond our current development to become stronger, more sensitive, and more creative in our search for high-quality lives.

The family of personal models pays great attention to the individual perspective and seeks to encourage productive independence, so that people become increasingly self-aware and responsible for their own destinies.

Personal models center on the development of self-actualizing individuals who understand themselves and can take charge of their future. As in the other families of models of teaching, the personal models differ in the specific aspects of personal development that they focus on.

FIGURE 2.2	Social Models	

MODEL	DEVELOPER (Redeveloper)	PURPOSE
Group Investigation	John Dewey Schlomo Sharan Rachel Hertz- Lazarowitz Herbert Thelen	Some would contend that this model can reach virtually any educational goal. Because many other models can be nested in it, it does, in fact, embrace a wide range of purposes. While preparing students for democratic life, it also helps them learn the modes of inquiry of the disciplines, teaches them to reflect on their own selves and values, and induces their commitment to the improvement of society.
Social Inquiry	Byron Massialas Benjamin Cox	Unites students in the study of social problems and provides them with strategies for doing so. Enhances social skills and fosters social commitment and logical thinking.
Jurisprudential Inquiry	James Shaver Donald Oliver	Helps students learn strategies for analyzing public issues with a jurisprudential framework. Increases students' awareness of social and personal values and skills for participating in democratic inquiry.
Laboratory Method	National Training Laboratory (many contributors)	Learning about group dynamics and developing strong, sensitive social skills is the forte of the laboratory method. Develops problem-solving skills, including some powerful strategies for resolving conflicts integratively and fairly.
Role-Playing	Fannie Shaftel George Shaftel	Inquiring into social and personal values is central. In addition, role-playing helps students develop strategies for understanding and resolving social problems ranging from conflict in small groups to conflicts in large communities.

FIGURE 2.2	Social Models *(continued)*

MODEL	DEVELOPER (Redeveloper)	PURPOSE
Positive Interdependence	David Johnson Roger Johnson Elizabeth Cohen	Oriented toward helping students learn interdependent strategies for social interaction, including the understanding of self-other relationships and emotions.
Structured Social Inquiry	Robert Slavin and colleagues	Directly helps students learn to cooperate in academic inquiry. In the process, fosters interpersonal skills, self-understanding, and commitment to excellence.

THE BEHAVIORAL SYSTEMS FAMILY

A common theoretical base—usually called social learning theory, but also known as behavior modification, behavior therapy, and cybernetics—guides the design of this family's models (see Figure 2.4 on p. 17). The belief is that human beings are self-correcting communication systems that modify behavior in response to information about how successfully they navigate tasks. For example, imagine a person climbing an unfamiliar staircase in the dark (the task). The first few steps are tentative, as a foot reaches for the treads. If the stride is too high, feedback is received as the foot encounters air and has to descend to make contact with the surface. If a step is too low, feedback results as the foot hits the riser. Gradually, the person adjusts behavior in accordance with the feedback until progress up the stairs is relatively comfortable.

Capitalizing on knowledge about how people respond to tasks and feedback, psychologists (see especially Skinner 1953) learned how to organize task and feedback structures to make it easy for human beings' self-correcting capability to function. Results include programs for reducing phobias; learning to read and compute; developing social and athletic skills; replacing anxiety with relaxation; and learning the complexities of intellectual, social, and physical skills necessary to pilot an airplane or a space shuttle. Because these models concentrate on observable behavior, clearly defined tasks, and methods for communicating progress to students, this family has a large foundation of research. Behavioral techniques are amenable to learners of all ages and to an impressive range of educational goals.

FIGURE 2.3   **Personal Models**

MODEL	DEVELOPER (Redeveloper)	PURPOSE
Nondirective Teaching	Carl Rogers	Building capacity for self-development is the focus. In the process, the model helps students understand themselves better, learn how to build their sense of self and self-worth, and strive for a high quality of life.
Awareness Training	Fritz Perls	Self-understanding and the capacity for exploration to enhance personal growth are the major purposes. Increased empathy and interpersonal sensitivity are also important. Making common cause for the development of all is fostered.
Classroom Meeting	William Glasser	Increases self-understanding and responsibility to self and others as inseparable sides of the developmental coin.
Self-Actualization	Abraham Maslow	Focuses on the development of self-understanding and increasing the capacity for personal development. In interpersonal settings, empathy and responsibility for others are corollary goals.
Conceptual Systems	David Hunt	Increases personal flexibility and complexity both in interacting with others and in the processing of information.

Behavioral systems models have shifted throughout the years from the development of "teaching systems" toward the development of environments where students learn how to learn. Thus, whereas 50 years ago, students might have been presented with a simulator designed to "teach" a group of complex skills, they are now taken to a simulation environment in which a person can, by responding productively to tasks and feedback, teach himself concepts and skills. Self-teaching capability is a major goal of all the behavioral systems models. Learning to assess performance, comprehend and respond to feedback, and adjust behavior to increase performance are subpurposes. The environments designed by the various behavioral models, however, differ considerably, and the emphasis they put on particular types of behaviors distinguish them from one another.

COMBINING APPROACHES ACROSS FAMILIES

These families of models are by no means antithetical or mutually exclusive, although each represents a distinctive approach to teaching. Whereas debates about educational method seem to imply that schools and teachers should choose one approach or another or no approach at all, students need growth in all areas. For example, to tend the personal but not the social, or the informational but not the personal, does not make sense in the life of a growing student.

USING THE TEACHING REPERTOIRE: A FIRM YET DELICATE HAND

In studying the four families, we try to build a mental picture of what each model is designed to accomplish and whether, under certain conditions, one is likely to have a larger effect than another. As we consider when and how to use various combinations of models and, therefore, which learning strategies will get priority for particular units, lessons, and groups of students, we consider the types and pace of learning that are likely to be promoted. To estimate a model's productivity, we draw

FIGURE 2.4	Behavioral Systems Models	

MODEL	DEVELOPER (Redeveloper)	PURPOSE
Social Learning	Albert Bandura Carl Thoresen Wes Becker Bill Mahoney	Helps students learn to study their behavior and its consequences and to try to develop more adaptive behavior by making changes and inquiring into their effects. Specific goals can be to reduce phobic and other dysfunctional patterns. Learning self-assessment and developing control are central purposes.
Mastery Learning	Benjamin Bloom James Block	The focus is to help students master academic content in all areas. The development of self-esteem and confidence through success is an important corollary purpose.
Programmed Learning	B.F. Skinner	Fostering the mastery of academic knowledge and skills is the purpose. Helping students assess growth and modify learning strategies is a corollary.
Simulation	Many developers Carl Smith and Mary Foltz Smith provide guide through 1960s when design had matured.	Helps students learn complex concepts and skills and assess development.
Direct Teaching	Thomas Good Jere Brophy Wes Becker Siegfried Englemann Carl Bereiter	Mastering academic knowledge and skills is the central purpose. Can also be used to develop strategies for learning in a wide variety of content areas.
Anxiety Reduction	David Rinn Joseph Wolpe John Masters	Learning to develop control over aversive emotional reactions is the central purpose. Teaches people self-treatment of avoidance and dysfunctional patterns of response.

on the research to help determine the types and extent of each model's effects.

Sometimes, decision making is relatively easy because one model stands out as though crafted for a given purpose. For example, the jurisprudential inquiry model teaches students how to analyze public issues. Therefore, it is most appropriate at the high school level and inappropriate with young children—young children don't study complex national and international political and economic issues either. A high school course that includes analyzing public issues as a primary objective can give major attention to the model, which can be used to design all or part of a course. The jurisprudential inquiry model also serves secondary objectives. For example, while studying issues, students learn information, concepts, and cooperative skills.

The decision is more complicated when several models can achieve the same objective. For example, information can be acquired through inductive inquiry or from readings and lectures developed around advance organizers. Or, the two models can be blended. Although a full discussion of how to coordinate models with objectives when designing curriculums, courses, and activities cannot be thoroughly addressed until the four families are studied, we need to keep in mind as we study each model that it eventually becomes part of a repertoire for designing programs of learning for our students. Effective education requires combinations of personal, social, and academic learning that can best be achieved by using several appropriate models.

Spaulding's (1970) work illustrates the importance of combining models in an educational program to pyramid their effects and achieve multiple objectives. Spaulding developed a program for economically poor, socially disruptive, low-achieving children, which used social learning theory techniques based on knowledge from developmental psychology and inductive teaching models. The program succeeded in improving students' social skills and cooperative learning behavior, induced students to take more responsibility for their education, substantially increased student learning of basic skills and knowledge, and even improved performances on tests of intelligence.

Placement as well as blending of models in a program of study is important. Consider a program to teach students a new language. One early task is to develop an initial vocabulary. Because the link-word method has been dramatically successful in initial vocabulary acquisition, in some cases helping students acquire and retain words twice as fast as normal (Pressley, Levin, and Delaney 1982), it's a good choice for use early in the program. Students need to acquire skills in reading, writing, and conversation, which are enhanced by an expanded vocabulary. Then, other models that generate practice and synthesis can be used.

To make matters even more complicated, we need to acknowledge, thankfully, that students are not identical. What helps one person learn a given thing more efficiently may not help another as much. Fortunately, there are few known cases showing that an educational treatment that helps one student a great deal has serious, damaging effects on another. But differences in positive effects can be substantial and need to be taken into account when designing educational environments. Thus, we pay attention to the "learning history" of students: how they have progressed academically and how they feel about themselves, their cognitive and personality development, and their social skills and attitudes.

Students change as their repertoire of learning strategies increases. And as they become a more powerful learning community, they can accomplish more types of learning more effectively. Increasing aptitude to learn is the fundamental purpose of teaching models.

The Information-Processing Family

The only way people come to appreciate the real power of the link-word method is to learn to use it themselves to learn new stuff—the more abstract and unfamiliar, the better. Folks can't just put it forward as something that is "good for the kids." You have to feel it to be able to teach it well. Come to think of it, maybe that's true of all the models.

—MIKE McKIBBIN TO BRUCE JOYCE
AUGUST 1980

SCENARIO I

At the Motilal Nehru School of Sports in the state of Haryana, India, two groups of 10th grade students are studying a botany unit that focuses on the structure of plant life. One group is using the textbook, with the tutorial help of the instructor, who illustrates the structures with plants found on the school grounds. We'll call this group the presentation-with-illustration group. The other group, which we'll call the inductive group, is taught by Bharati Baveja, an instructor at Delhi University. The second group is given a large number of plants labeled with the plant names. Working in pairs, Ms. Baveja's students build classifications of the plants, which are based on the structural characteristics of plant

20

roots, stems, and leaves. Periodically, the pairs share and generate labels for their classifications.

Occasionally, Ms. Baveja employs concept attainment to introduce a concept designed to expand the students' frame of reference and induce more complex classification. She also supplies the scientific names for the categories the students invent. Eventually, Ms. Baveja presents new specimens and asks students to see if they can predict the structure of one plant part from observing another part—for example, predicting the root structure from observing the leaves. Finally, she asks them to collect more specimens and fit them into the categories they have developed so they can determine how comprehensive their categories have become. They discover that most of the new plants fit into existing categories; a few need new categories.

After two weeks of study, the two groups take a unit test in which they are asked to analyze more specimens and name structural characteristics. Compared to the presentation-with-illustration group, the inductive group gained twice as much on the test of knowledge and correctly identified the structure of eight times more specimens.

SCENARIO II

Jack Wilson is a 1st grade teacher in Lincoln, Nebraska. He meets daily for reading instruction with a group of children who are progressing well. He is concerned, however, because they sometimes have trouble attacking new words when they can't figure out the meaning from the context. If they can figure out what a word means from the rest of the sentence, they are able to use principles they have learned to sound the words out. Mr. Wilson has concluded that they don't have full control over phonetic and structural analysis concepts and principles. To help them develop concepts of how words are structured and to use that knowledge in attacking new words, he plans a series of activities over the next several weeks.

Mr. Wilson prepares a deck of cards, one word on each card. He selects words that have particular prefixes and suffixes and the same root word. He picks prefixes and suffixes because they are prominent structural characteristics of words, making them easy to identify. (Later, he'll add more subtle phonetic and structural features.) Here are some pairs of words with and without prefixes:

| set | reset | heat | preheat | plant | replant |
| run | rerun | set | preset | plan | preplan |

When the group of students convenes on Monday morning, Mr. Wilson gives several cards to each student. He keeps the remainder, planning to gradually increase the amount of information students receive. Mr. Wilson asks each student to read a word on a card and describe something about the word. Other students may add to the description. This activity brings the structural properties of the word to the students' attention. The discussion surfaces such features as initial consonants (e.g., begins with *s)*, vowels, and pairs of consonants (e.g., *pl).*

After the students become familiar with the assortment of words, Mr. Wilson instructs, "Put the words that go together in piles." The students begin studying their cards, passing them back and forth as they sort out the commonalities.

At first, the card piles reflect only the initial letters or the meanings of the words, such as whether the words refer to motion or warmth. Gradually, the students notice the prefixes and how they are spelled. They look up the prefixes in the dictionary and discover how adding a prefix affects the meaning of a root word.

When the students finish sorting the words, Mr. Wilson asks them to talk about each category, telling what the cards have in common. Gradually, because of the way Mr. Wilson has selected the data, the students discover the major prefixes and suffixes and reflect on their meaning. Then, he gives them sentences that include words not in their deck and that contain prefixes and suffixes they have learned. He asks them to figure out the meanings of those words, applying the concepts they have formed to help them unlock the meanings.

This inductive activity is conducted many times. By selecting different sets of words, Mr. Wilson leads the students through the categories of consonant and vowel sounds and structures they need to attack unfamiliar words, studying their progress and adjusting the classification tasks when needed.

SCENARIO III

Eight-year-old Seamus appears to be playing in his kitchen. In front of him are a number of plates. On one is a potato, cut in quarters; on another, an apple, similarly cut. The other plates contain various fruits and vegetables. Seamus pushes into the potato segments some copper and zinc plates, which are wired together and to a tiny light bulb. He nods with satisfaction when the bulb begins to glow. He disconnects the bulb, attaches a voltmeter, examines it briefly, and then reattaches the bulb. He repeats the process with the apple, examining the bulb and voltmeter once again. Then come the raspberries, lemon, carrot, and remaining foods. His father enters the room. Seamus looks up.

"I was right about the raspberries," he says. "We can use them as in a battery. But, some of these other things . . . ."

Seamus is, of course, classifying fruits and vegetables according to whether or not they can interact with metals to produce electric current.

SCENARIO IV

Diane Schuetz provided her 1st grade students with sets of tulip bulbs, which they classified. The students based their groupings on size, whether two were joined together ("some have babies on them"), whether they had "coats," and whether they had the beginnings of what looked like roots. Now the students are planting their bulbs to find out if the variation in attributes they identified affects how the tulips grow: "Will the big ones [bulbs] grow bigger?" "Will the babies grow on their own?" Ms. Schuetz designed the science curriculum around the basic processes of building categories, making predictions, and testing their validity.

SCENARIO V

Dr. Makibbin's social studies class is examining data from a large demographic base on the nations of the world. One group of students is looking at the base on Africa; another is studying Latin America; and the others are pouring over data from Asia and Europe. They are searching for correlations among variables, such as whether per capita income is associated with life expectancy and whether educational level is associated with rate of increase in population. As they share the results of their inquiry, they will compare the nations, trying to learn if the correlations within each are comparable to the others.

COMMENTARY ON SCENARIOS

These five teachers use essentially the same process, with content from several curriculum areas and with primary and secondary school children. In each case, the process objectives (learning to build, test, and use categories) are combined with the content objectives (inquiring into and mastering important topics in the curriculum).

THE INFORMATION-PROCESSING MODELS OF TEACHING

Focusing directly on intellectual capability, information-processing models help students learn how to construct knowledge. As the term implies, information-processing models help students operate on information obtained either from direct experience or from mediated sources so that they develop conceptual control over the areas they study. The emphases of the various information-processing models are somewhat different; however, each is designed to enhance particular kinds of thinking.

Inductive Thinking Model

The inductive thinking model induces students to collect and classify information and to build and test hypotheses. Classification, which is one phase of this model, is probably the basic higher-order thinking skill and is necessary for mastering large amounts of information.

Concept Attainment Model

The concept attainment model helps students learn concepts and study how they think. Simultaneously, it leads students to develop concepts and obtain conceptual control (metacognitive understanding) over their thinking strategies.

Synectics Model

The synectics model teaches metaphoric thinking—ways of consciously breaking set (backing off from routine thinking) and generating new ideas.

Scientific Inquiry Models

The scientific inquiry models bring students an understanding of how scholars collect and analyze information by taking students through inquiries modeled after the modes of inquiry of the academic disciplines.

Inquiry Training Model

Inquiry training specializes in causal reasoning, thus sharpening the tools of scientific inquiry.

Cognitive Growth

This model is used to assess students' intellectual maturity and to design experiences to "pull" cognitive growth along. For example, if students' thinking about social relations is purely egocentric, experiences are provided to help them think about self and others simultaneously.

Advance Organizer Model

The advance organizer model helps students become active learners in situations where they receive information through lectures and written assignments. They learn to strive for the conceptual structures of the content, which enable them to organize information and make it their own.

Mnemonics Models

The recently developed mnemonics models have raised the process of memorizing to a surprisingly high conceptual level by providing tools to help students learn and analyze information and gain conscious control of their learning processes and how those processes can be improved.

For maximum effect, these models are used in combinations as students learn to inquire into any given topic. The inductive thinking model can help students collect and analyze information; concept attainment helps them develop new perspectives on the data. Synectics helps students stretch their ideas and reformulate them. And mnemonics can help students anchor information and ideas in their long-term memory.

THE INDUCTIVE THINKING MODEL AS AN ILLUSTRATION

The five scenarios that introduced this chapter illustrate the inductive thinking model in operation. As with the other more powerful and utilitarian models of teaching, such as group investigation in the social family, the inductive thinking model has a long history. Inductive thinking has been written about since the classical Greek period; during the last 30 years, the model for it has been polished and studied formally. Current classroom use is influenced by the work of Hilda Taba (1966), who was largely responsible for popularizing the term *teaching strategy* and for shaping the inductive thinking model so that it can easily be used to design curriculums and lessons.

The inductive thinking model helps students learn to collect and examine information closely, organize it into concepts, and manipulate those concepts. Used regularly, this strategy increases both students' abilities to form concepts efficiently and the range of perspectives from which they can view information.

If a group of students regularly engages in inductive thinking activity, the group can be taught to use increasing numbers of sources for data. The students can learn to examine data from many sides and scrutinize all aspects of objects and events. For example, imagine students studying communities. We can expect that, at first, their data will be superficial, but their increasingly sophisticated inquiry will turn up more and more attributes that they can use for classifying the information they are gathering. Also, if a classroom of students works in groups to form concepts and data and the groups share the categories they develop, they will stimulate each other to look at the information from different perspectives.

RESEARCH

Although much research on information-processing models has been focused on how to increase students' ability to form and use concepts and hypotheses, both practitioners and laypeople ask a number of relevant questions, reflecting a concern that a concentration on thinking may inhibit mastery of content. Teachers phrase the concern like this: "I have much content to cover. If I devote energy to the teaching of thinking, won't students miss out on the basic skills and content that are the core of the curriculum?" Several research reviews address this question:

• El-Nemr (1979) concentrated on the teaching of biology with the inductive thinking and scientific inquiry models in high schools and colleges. He looked at the effects on student achievement, development of process skills, and attitudes toward science. The experimentally oriented biology curriculums achieved positive effects on all three outcomes. The average effect sizes are largest for process skills (0.44 at the high school level and 0.62 at the college level). For achievement, they are 0.27 and 0.11, respectively, and for attitudes, 0.22 and 0.51. (See Appendix for an explanation of "effect size" and how to interpret it.)

• Bredderman's (1983) analysis included a broader range of science programs plus the elementary grades. He also reports positive effects for information acquisition (0.10), creativity (0.13), and science process (0.52). In addition, he reports effects on intelligence tests when they were included (0.50).

• Hillocks's (1987) review of the teaching of writing produced similar results. His conclusion indicates how closely how we teach is connected to what we teach. Essentially, the inductive, inquiry-oriented approaches to the teaching of writing produce average effect sizes of about 0.60, compared to treatments that cover the same material but without the inductive approaches to the teaching/learning process.

• Other researchers approached the question of coverage by examining the transfer of the teaching of thinking from one curriculum to another. They found that inquiry-oriented curriculums appear to stimulate growth in other, apparently unconnected, areas. For example, Smith's (1980) analysis of aesthetics curriculums shows that implementation of the arts-oriented curriculums is accompanied by gains in the basic skills areas.

Time and efficiency were recently addressed in a number of large-scale field studies in the basic curriculum areas. One study involved the 190 elementary school teachers in an Iowa school district. Teachers and administrators focused on improving the quality of student writing by using the inductive thinking model of teaching. Students explored the techniques that published authors used to accomplish tasks such as introducing characters, establishing settings, and describing action. At intervals, teachers collected writing samples, which were scored by experts who did not know the children's identity.

By the end of the year, student writing had dramatically improved. End-of-year scores for writing quality were higher for 4th grade students than end-of year scores for 8th grade students the previous year! Students had made greater gains in one year than were normally achieved by comparable students over a period of four years. Moreover, students at all levels of writing quality gained substantially—from those who started with the poorest writing skills to those who began with the most developed skills. A gender gap in writing (i.e., males often lag behind females in developing writing skills) narrowed significantly (Joyce, Calhoun, Carran, Halliburton, Simser, and Rust 1994; Joyce, Calhoun, Carran, Simser, Rust, and Halliburton 1996).

Figure 3.1 (see p. 29) shows student improvement in 4th grade. The table compares the means for two periods (fall 1992 and spring 1993) for three dimensions (focus/organization, support, and grammar/mechanics). In the fall, coefficients of correlation between the dimensions of focus/organization and support were 0.56; between the dimensions of focus/organization and grammar/mechanics, 0.61; and between the dimensions of support and grammar/mechanics, 0.63. In the spring, these were 0.84, 0.65, and 0.74, respectively.

Effect sizes were computed for fall and spring scores: for focus/organization, 2.18; for support, 1.53; and for grammar/mechanics, 1.37. These effect sizes are several times the effect sizes calculated for a year's gain for the national sample and for the baseline gains determined from the 1991–92 analyses in that Iowa district. For focus/organization, the differences are so great that in the spring, the average student reached the top of the fall distribution, something that does not happen nationally during the entire time from grades 4 to 12.

FIGURE 3.1	Comparison of 4th Grade Fall 1992 and Spring 1993 Mean Scores on Expository Writing

	D i m e n s i o n s		
Period	**Focus/ Organization**	Support	**Grammar/ Mechanics**
Fall 1992	1.60	2.20	2.11
Mean	0.55	0.65	0.65
Standard Deviation			
Spring 1993	2.80	3.20	3.00
Mean	0.94	0.96	0.97
Standard Deviation			

Source: Joyce, Calhoun, Carran, Simser, Rust, and Halliburton 1996.

That the same model of teaching reached all the students is surprising to many, but the finding is typical in studies of teaching and teaching strategies. Teachers who "reach" students having poor histories of learning and help them out of their rut also propel the best students into higher states of growth than the students have been accustomed to.

❖   ❖   ❖

Students of all ages can process information richly. It is sometimes thought that higher-order thinking is reserved for the mature. Not so. Although the content of primary education needs to be rich with concrete experience, little kids can learn to think well, too. Similarly, complex, inquiry-oriented models of instruction have turned out to be the best educational medicine for students who start school slowly or later have the poorest learning histories.

Old fencing masters used to tell their students that you grip the sword as you would hold a sparrow: If you hold it too tightly, it cannot breathe. If you hold it too loosely, it will fly away.

Good thinking is analogous to a fencer's grip, combining discipline with flexibility. If we are to help children become more powerful and flexible thinkers, we have to master the paradox and create environments that offer challenge and strong support, without smothering the very characteristics we seek to nurture.

The Social Family

The most stunning thing about teaching people to help kids learn cooperatively is that people don't know how to do it as a consequence of their own schooling and life in this society. And, if anything is genetically driven, it's a social instinct. If it weren't for each other, we wouldn't even know who we are.

—HERBERT THELEN TO BRUCE JOYCE
CIRCA 1964

SCENARIO I

Debbie Psychoyos's 11th grade social studies class on world geography has been studying demographic data taken from the computer program PCGLOBE on 205 nations of the world. Each of the nine groups of four students has analyzed the data on 20 nations and searched for correlations among the following variables: population, per capita GNP (gross national product), birth rate, life expectancy, education, health care services, industrial base, agricultural production, transportation systems, foreign debt, balance of payments, women's rights, and natural resources.

The groups reported, and what had begun as a purely academic exercise suddenly aroused the students:

31

"People born in some countries have a life expectancy 20 years less than folks in other countries."

"We didn't find a relationship between levels of education and per capita wealth!"

"Some rich countries spend more on military facilities and personnel than some large poor ones spend on health care!"

"Women's rights don't correlate with type of government! Some democracies are less liberal than some dictatorships!"

"Some little countries are relatively wealthy because of commerce and industry. Some others just have one mineral that is valuable."

"The United States owes other countries an awful lot of money."

The time is ripe for group investigation. Ms. Psychoyos carefully leads the students to record their reactions to the data. They make a decision to bring together the data on all the countries and find out if the conclusions the groups are forming will hold over the entire data set. They also decide that they need to find a way of getting in-depth information about selected countries to flesh out their statistical data. But which countries? How will they test their hypotheses?

One student wonders aloud about world organizations and how they relate to the social situation of the world. Similar concerns and questions are voiced by others:

• The class has heard of the United Nations and UNESCO but are vague about how they function.

• One student has heard about the "Committee of Seven."

• Several have heard of NATO but are not sure how it operates.

• Several wonder about the European Economic Community.

• Many wonder about the dissolution of the USSR and what it will mean.

• Several wonder about China and its immense population and how it fits into the global picture.

Clearly, deciding priorities for the inquiry will not be easy. The conditions for group investigation, however, are present. The students are puzzled. They react differently to the various questions. They need information, and information sources are available.

Ms. Psychoyos smiles at her brood of young furrowed brows. "Let's get organized. There is information we all need, and let's start with that.

Then let's prioritize our questions and divide the labor to get information that will help us."

SCENARIO II

As the children enter Kelly Farmer's 5th grade classroom in Savannah Elementary on the first day of school, they find the class roster on each desk.

Ms. Farmer smiles at her students and says, "Let's start by learning all our names and one of the ways we will be working together this year. You'll notice I've arranged the desks in pairs, and the persons sitting at each pair will be partners in today's activities. I want each partnership to take our class list and classify the first names by how they sound. Then we will share the groupings or categories each partnership makes. This activity will help us learn one another's names. It will also introduce you to one of the ways we will study spelling and several other subjects this year. I know from Ms. Annis that you worked inductively last year so you know how to classify information, but let me know if you have any problems."

The students *do* know what to do, and within a few minutes, they are ready to share their classifications:

"We put *Nancy* and *Sally* together because they end in *y*."

"We put *George* and *Jerry* together because they sound the same at the beginning although they're spelled differently."

"We put the three *Kevin*'s together."

A few minutes later, the pairs are murmuring as they help one another learn to spell the list of names.

Ms. Farmer has started the year by organizing the students into a cooperative set, an organization for cooperative learning. She will teach the students to work in dyads and triads, which can be combined into groups of five or six (task or work groups larger than five or six generally have much lower productivity). The partnerships will change, depending on the activity. The students will learn to accept any members of the class as their partners and understand that they are to work with each other to try to ensure that everyone achieves the objectives of each activity.

Ms. Farmer begins with pairs because that is the simplest social organization. In fact, much of the early training in cooperative activity will be conducted in groups of two and three because the interaction is simpler than it is in larger groups. She also uses fairly straightforward and familiar cognitive tasks for the initial training for the same reason— it is easier for students to learn to work together when they are not mastering complex activities at the same time. For example, she will ask them to change partners and have the new partnerships quiz each other on simple knowledge, such as facts about the states and their capitals, and tutor one another. After the students change partners again, she will ask them to categorize sets of fractions by size. A variety of tasks will help each student learn how to work with all the other students in the class. Later, Ms. Farmer will teach the children to respond to the cognitive tasks of the more complex information-processing models of teaching, as well as more complex cooperative sets. By the end of October, she expects the students to be skillful enough that she can introduce them to group investigation.

COMMENTARY ON SCENARIOS

Both teachers—one working with 11th graders and one working with 5th graders—have embarked on the task of building learning communities. Both will teach the students to work together impersonally but positively, to gather and analyze information, to build and test hypotheses, and to coach one another as they develop skills. The difference in maturity between the classes affects the degree of sophistication of their inquiry, but the basic teaching-learning process is the same.

Each teacher uses different strategies for helping their students learn to work productively together. On the teachers' desks are *Learning Together and Alone* (Johnson and Johnson 1994) and *Cooperative Learning Resources for Teachers* (Kagan 1990). Both teachers are studying their students, learning how effectively they cooperate, and deciding how to design the next activities to teach them to work more effectively together.

THE SOCIAL MODELS OF TEACHING

As stated in Chapter 2, working together generates collective energy, or synergy. The social models of teaching make the most of this phenomenon by building learning communities. Models in this family include group investigation (the most complex form of cooperative learning), jurisprudential inquiry, and role-playing. Let's briefly look at these three models.

Group Investigation Model

Group investigation is a direct route to developing a community of learners. All the simpler forms of cooperative learning are preparation for the rigorous, active, and integrative collective action required in group investigation. John Dewey (1916) developed the idea; teachers and theorists extended and refined it; and Herbert Thelen (1960) shaped it into a powerful definition: *Education in a democratic society should teach democratic process directly.* A substantial part of students' education should involve cooperative inquiry into important social and academic problems. The group investigation model provides a social organization within which many other models can be used.

Group investigation has been used in all subject areas, with children of all ages, and even as the core social model for entire schools (Chamberlin and Chamberlin 1943). The model leads students to define problems; explore perspectives on the problems; and study together to master information, ideas, and skills—while simultaneously developing social competence. The teacher's primary role is to help organize and discipline the group process, help students find and organize information, and ensure that a vigorous level of activity and discourse occurs.

Jurisprudential Inquiry Model

As students mature, they are able to study social issues at community, state, national, and international levels. The jurisprudential inquiry model is designed for this purpose. Created especially for secondary students in the social studies, the model brings the case-study method, reminiscent of legal education, to the process of schooling (Oliver and Shaver 1971, Shaver 1995). Students study cases involving social problems in areas where public policy needs to be made (e.g., on issues of justice and equality, poverty and power). They are led to identify the public policy issues, the options available for dealing with the issues, and the values underlying those options. Although developed for the social studies, this model can be used in any area where there are public policy issues. Most curriculum areas abound with them (e.g., ethics in science, business, and sports).

Role-Playing Model

Role-playing leads students to understand social behavior, their roles in social interactions, and ways of solving problems more effectively. Designed by Fannie and George Shaftel (1982) specifically to help students study their social values and reflect on them, role-playing also helps students collect and organize information about social issues, develop empathy with others, and attempt to improve their social skills. The model asks students to act out conflicts, to learn to take the roles of others, and to observe social behavior. With appropriate adaptation, role-playing can be used with students of all ages.

Cooperative Learning Models

In this section, we share some of the research underpinning the social family of models, of which group investigation is the most complex form, and look more closely at the uses of role-playing as a teaching-learning strategy.

Three lines of research have developed on ways of helping students study and learn together: one led by David and Roger Johnson, one led by Robert Slavin, and one led by Shlomo and Yael Sharan and Rachel Hertz-Lazarowitz in Israel.

The Johnsons and their colleagues (Johnson and Johnson 1981, 1989) studied the effects of cooperative tasks and reward structures on learning. Their work (Johnson and Johnson 1981, 1994) on peers teaching peers has provided information about the effects of cooperative behavior both on traditional learning tasks and on values and intergroup behavior and attitudes. Their models emphasize the development of what they call positive interdependence, or cooperation where collective action also celebrates individual differences.

Slavin's extensive review (1983) includes a study of various approaches in which he manipulates the complexity of social tasks in various types of groupings. He reports success in heterogeneous groups with tasks requiring coordination of group members both on academic learning and intergroup relations, and he has generated a variety of strategies that employ extrinsic and intrinsic reward structures.

The Israeli team, led by Shlomo Sharan, concentrated on group investigation, the most complex of the social models of teaching.

What is the magnitude of effects that we can expect when we learn to use cooperative learning strategies effectively? (See the Appendix for an explanation of "effect size.") Rolheiser-Bennett's study (1986) compares the effects of the degrees of cooperative structure required by the several approaches that cooperative learning specialists have generated (Joyce, Showers, and Rolheiser-Bennett 1987). On standardized tests in the basic curriculum areas (such as reading and mathematics), the highly structured approaches to teaching students to work together generated effect sizes of an average 0.28, with some studies approaching half a standard deviation in effects. On criterion-referenced tests, the average effect size was 0.48, with some of the best implementations reaching an effect of about one standard deviation. The more elaborate cooperative learning models generated an average effect size of more than one standard deviation, with some exceeding two standard deviations. (The average student was above the 90th percentile student in the control group.) The effects on higher-order thinking were even greater, with an average effect of about 1.25 standard deviations and effects in some studies as high as three standard deviations.

Taken as a whole, research on cooperative learning is overwhelmingly positive—nearly every study has shown modest to very high effects. Moreover, the cooperative approaches are effective over a range of achievement measures. The more intensely cooperative the environment, the greater the effects; the more complex the outcomes (i.e., higher-order processing of information and problem solving), the greater the effects.

The cooperative environment engendered by the cooperative learning models has had substantial benefits:

- Increased the cooperative behavior of students.
- Increased feelings of empathy for others.
- Reduced intergroup tensions and aggressive and antisocial behavior.

- Improved moral judgment.
- Increased positive feelings toward others, including those of other ethnic groups.

Many of the effect sizes reported are substantial—one or two standard deviations are not uncommon for academic learning, and social learning effects have been remarkable in some cases. Hertz-Lazarowitz (1993) recently used one of the cooperative learning models to create integrative interaction between Israeli and Arab students in the West Bank! Margarita Calderon has worked with Hertz-Lazarowitz and Tinajero (Calderon, Hertz-Lazarowitz, and Tinajero 1991) to adapt a cooperative integrated reading and composition program for bilingual students, with some impressive results. In higher education, organizing students into cooperative study groups reduced a dropout rate in engineering from 40 percent to about 5 percent (Bonsangue 1993). Conflict resolution strategies taught students to develop integrative behavior and reduced social tension in divided environments in inner-city schools.

Information is also available on whole school cooperative learning. Research that compares schools has continued for some time. In the early years, these studies were designed on a planned variation model, where schools operating from different stances toward education were compared with one another. For example, 50 years ago, the beautifully designed "eight-year study" submitted the theses of the "progressive movement" (largely cooperative learning oriented) to a serious (and generally successful) test and defended it against the suggestion that social and personal models of education were dangerous to the academic health of students (Chamberlin and Chamberlin 1943). Recent research on unusually effective schools finds that one of their most prominent characteristics is a cooperative social climate in which all faculty and students work together to build a supportive, achievement-oriented climate.

A group of secondary school teachers in Israel, led by Shlomo Sharan and Hana Shachar (1988), demonstrated the rapid acceleration of student learning when they studied and began to use the group investigation model. These teachers worked with classes in which children of the poor (referred to as "low SES," shorthand for "lower socioeconomic status") were mixed with children of middle class parents (referred to as "high SES," for "higher socioeconomic status"). In a yearlong course on the social studies, the teachers gave students pre-tests as well as final examinations to measure gains in academic learning and to compare the gains with those of students taught by the whole class format most common in Israeli schools. The table (Figure 4.1) shows the results.

FIGURE 4.1	Effects of Complex Cooperative Learning in a History Course			
	Cooperative Learning (Treatment)[1]		Whole Class Control	
	High SES[2]	Low SES	High SES	Low SES
Pre-Test				
M	20.99	14.81	21.73	12.31
SD	9.20	7.20	10.53	7.05
Post-Test				
M	62.60	50.17	42.78	27.23
SD	10.85	14.44	14.40	13.73
Mean Gain	41.61	35.36	21.05	14.92

[1]The group investigation model of teaching was used.
[2]SES refers to socioeconomic status.
Source: Sharan and Shachar 1988.

You can make several interesting comparisons as you read the table. First, in the pre-tests, the lower SES students scored significantly lower than their higher SES counterparts. (Typically, socioeconomic status is related to the knowledge that students bring to the instructional situation, and these students were no exception.) The lower SES students taught by teachers using the group investigation model achieved average gains nearly two and a half times those of the lower SES students taught by teachers using the whole class method *and* exceeded the scores made by the higher SES students taught by teachers using the whole class format. In other words, the "socially disadvantaged" students taught using the group investigation model learned at rates above those of the "socially advantaged" students taught by teachers who did not have the repertoire that the group investigation model provides. Finally, the "advantaged" students also learned more through group investigation. Their average gain was *twice* that of their whole class counterparts. Thus, the model was effective by a large margin for students from both backgrounds.

THE ROLE-PLAYING MODEL AS AN ILLUSTRATION

We placed role-playing in the social family of models because the social group plays such an indispensable part in human development and because of the unique opportunity that role-playing offers for resolving interpersonal and social dilemmas. Role-playing has roots in both the personal and social dimensions of education: It attempts to help individuals find personal meaning within their social worlds and to resolve personal dilemmas with the assistance of the social group. In the social dimension, role-playing allows individuals to work together in analyzing social situations, especially interpersonal problems, and in developing decent and democratic ways of coping with these situations.

We selected the role-playing model as our example from the social family to illustrate alternative ways of building a learning community in the classroom. In role-playing, students explore human relations problems by enacting problem situations then discussing the enactments. Together, students can explore feelings, attitudes, values, and problem-solving strategies.

Several teams of researchers experimented with role-playing, and their treatments of the strategy are remarkably similar. The version we use in the following scenario was formulated by Fannie and George Shaftel (1982). We also incorporated ideas from the work of Mark Chesler and Robert Fox (1966).

Scenario

We are in a 7th grade classroom in East Los Angeles, California. After recess, the students have returned to the classroom and are complaining excitedly to one another. Mr. Williams, the teacher, asks what the matter is, and they all talk at once, discussing a series of difficulties that lasted throughout recess. Apparently, two students began to squabble about who was to take the sports equipment outside. Then, all the students argued about what game to play. Next, there was a dispute about choosing sides for the games, including a disagreement about whether the girls should be included with the boys or play separately. The class finally began to play volleyball. Almost immediately, players began arguing over a line call, and the game was never completed.

At first, Mr. Williams displays his displeasure toward the class. He is angry, not simply over the incidents, but because these arguments have been going on since the beginning of the year.

At last he says, "Okay, we really have to face this problem. You must be as tired of it as I am, and you really are not acting maturely. So we are going to use a technique that we have been using to discuss family problems to approach our own problems right here in this classroom: We're going to use role-playing. Now I want you to divide into groups and try to identify the types of problems that we've been having. Just take today, for example, and outline the problem situations that got us into this fix."

The students begin with the argument over taking the sports equipment outside, and then outline other arguments. Each is a situation that students typically face and must learn to take a stand on. After the student groups have listed their problems, Mr. Williams appoints one student to lead a class discussion in which each group reports the kinds of problem situations that have come up; the groups agree on a half-dozen problems that have consistently bothered the class.

The students then group the problems according to type. One type concerns the division of labor; a second deals with deciding principles for selecting teams; and a third focuses on resolving disputes over the particulars of games, such as whether balls have been hit out of bounds and whether players are out or safe. Mr. Williams then assigns one type of problem to each group and asks the groups to describe situations in which the problems occur. When the groups are finished, the class votes on which problem to start with. They select disputes over rules, and the actual problem situation they select is the volleyball game in which the dispute over a line call occurred.

Together, the class discusses how the problem situation develops. It begins when a ball is hit close to the boundary line. One team believes the ball is in, and the other believes it is out of bounds. The students then argue with one another, and the argument goes on so that the game cannot continue.

Several students are selected to enact the situation. Others gather around and are assigned to observe particular aspects of the role-playing that follows. Some students are to look for the particulars of how the argument develops. Some are to study one role-player and others another to determine how the actors handle the situation.

The enactment is spirited. The students select as role-players those who have been on opposite sides during the game, and the actors become as involved in the argument during the role-playing as they were during the actual situation. Finally, they are standing in the middle of the room shouting at one another.

At this point, Mr. Williams calls, "Time!" and asks the students to describe what has gone on.

Everyone is eager to talk. The discussion gradually focuses on how the attitude of the participants prevented resolving the problem. No one was listening to the other person, and no one was dealing with the problem of how to resolve honest disputes. Finally, Mr. Williams asks the students to suggest other ways that people could behave in this kind of conflict. Some students suggest giving in gracefully. But others object that if someone believes she is right, giving in is not an easy thing to do.

Finally, the students identify an important question on which to focus: "How can we develop a policy about who should make calls, and how should others feel about those calls?"

They decide to reenact the scene by having the participants assume that the defensive team should make the calls only when members see clear evidence that a ball is out and the other team has not seen the evidence.

The reenactment takes place. This time, the players attempt to follow the policy that the defensive team has the right to make a call, but the offensive team has the right to object to a call. Once again, the enactment results in a shouting match; however, after it is over, the students observing the enactment point out that the role-players do not behave as if there were a resolution to the situation. The class recognizes that if there are to be games, there has to be agreement about who can make calls and a certain amount of trust on both sides.

The class decides to try a third enactment, this time with two new role-players added as dispute referees. The introduction of referees completely changes the third enactment. The referees insist that the other players pay attention to them, which the players do not want to do. In discussing this enactment, the students point out that a system is needed to ensure reasonable order and the resolution of disputes. The students also agree that as things stand, they probably are unable to re-solve disputes without including a referee of some sort, but that no ref-erees will be effective unless the students agree to accept the referees' decisions as final. The class decides that in future games, two students will be referees, chosen by lottery prior to the game. Their function will be to arbitrate and make all calls relevant to the rules of the game, and their decisions will be final. The students agree that they will see how that system works.

The next day, Mr. Williams opens up the second set of issues, and the students repeat this process. Exploring other areas of dispute con-tinues over the next few weeks. At first, many of the notions that are clarified are simply practical ones about how to solve specific problems. Gradually, however, Mr. Williams directs the discussion to a considera-tion of the basic values governing individual behavior. The students be-gin to see the problems of communal living, and they develop policies for governing their own behavior, as individuals and as a group. They also begin to develop skills in negotiating. The students who were locked in conflict gradually learn that if they behave in a slightly differ-ent way, others may also modify their behavior, and problems become easier to solve.

Goals and Assumptions of Role-Playing

On its simplest level, role-playing is dealing with problems through action: A problem is delineated, acted out, and discussed. Some stu-dents are role-players, and others are observers. The role-players put themselves in the positions of other people and then try to interact with each other. As empathy, sympathy, anger, and affection are all gener-ated during the interaction, role-playing, if done well, becomes a part of life. This emotional content, as well as the words and the actions, be-comes part of the later analysis. When the acting out is finished, even the observers are involved enough to want to know why the role-players reached their decision, what the sources of resistance were, and whether there were other ways this situation could have been approached.

The essence of role-playing is the involvement of participants and observers in a real problem situation and the desire for resolution and understanding that this involvement engenders. The role-playing process provides a live sample of human behavior that serves as a vehicle for students to (1) explore their feelings; (2) gain insight into their attitudes, values, and perceptions; (3) develop their problem-solving skills and attitudes; and (4) explore subject matter in varied ways.

These goals reflect several assumptions about the learning process in role-playing. First, role-playing implicitly advocates an experience-based learning situation in which the here and now becomes the content of instruction. The model assumes that creating authentic analogies to real-life problem situations is possible and that through these re-creations students can sample life. Thus, the enactment elicits genuine, typical emotional responses and behaviors from the students.

A second and related assumption is that role-playing can draw out students' feelings, which they can recognize and perhaps release. The Shaftels' version of role-playing emphasizes the intellectual content as much as the emotional content: Analysis and discussion of the enactment are as important as the role-playing itself. As educators, we are concerned that students recognize and understand their feelings and see how their feelings influence their behavior.

A third assumption is that the emotions and ideas of individuals can be brought to consciousness and enhanced by the group structure. The collective reactions of members of the peer group can bring out new ideas and provide directions for growth and change. The model de-emphasizes the traditional role of teacher and encourages listening and learning from one's peers.

A fourth and final assumption is that covert psychological processes involving one's attitudes, values, and belief system can be brought to consciousness by combining spontaneous enactment with analysis. Furthermore, individuals can gain some control over their belief systems if they can recognize their values and attitudes and test them against the views of others. Such analysis can help individuals evaluate their attitudes and values and the consequences of their beliefs so that they can allow themselves to grow.

Social models draw on the energy of a group and capitalize on common cause and the potential that comes from differing points of view and orientations. The core objective is to help students learn to work together to identify and solve problems.

The Personal Family

The idea that you teach kids how to ask and answer questions, rather than just asking them questions, came as a revelation to me.

—A TEACHER OF 20 YEARS TO BRUCE JOYCE
MAY 1995

From birth, we are acted on by the world. Our social environment gives us our language, teaches us how to behave, and provides love. But our individual selves configure themselves relentlessly and create their own interior environments. Within these interior worlds, each of us creates our identity, and our personalities have remarkable continuity from early in life (White 1978).

Although much within our interior world remains stable, we also have great capacity to change. We are incomplete without others and can give and receive love, which perhaps generates the greatest growth of all. Paradoxically, we also have the capacity to hold tight to behavior that doesn't work—as if to force the world to yield and make our worst features productive. We can adapt to a wide range of environments. We are the greatest! And, we can be mulish!

46

The personal models of teaching emphasize the unique character of each human being and the struggle to develop as an integrated, confident, and competent personality. The goal is to help each person "own" his development and achieve a sense of self-worth and personal harmony. The models that comprise this family seek to develop and integrate the emotional and intellectual aspects of personality.

THE NONDIRECTIVE TEACHING MODEL AS AN ILLUSTRATION

From the range of personal models, we selected Carl Rogers's (1982) nondirective teaching model to illustrate the philosophy and techniques of the personal family. Two scenarios show how two teachers used the model to deal with the organization of the classroom as a self-disciplining community of learners.

Scenario I: Using the Model with the Class as a Unit

An important use of nondirective teaching occurs when a class becomes stale and the teacher finds herself just pushing the students through exercises and subject matter. Karla Trobaugh, a 6th grade teacher exhausted by the failure of traditional attempts to cope with discipline problems and class disinterest, decided to experiment with student-centered teaching. She turned to nondirective approaches to help her students take more responsibility for their learning and to ensure that the subject matter would be related to their needs and learning styles. She provided an account of that experience; excerpts are presented here.

March 5, We Begin. A week ago, I decided to initiate a new program in my 6th grade classroom, based on student-centered teaching—an unstructured or nondirective approach. I began by telling the class that we were going to try an experiment. For one day, I would let them do anything they wanted to do—they did not have to do anything they did not want to do.

Many students started with art projects; some drew or painted for most of the day. Others read or did work in math and other subjects.

Excitement was in the air all day. Many were so interested in what they were doing that they did not want to go out at recess!

At the end of the day, I asked the class to evaluate the experiment. The comments were most interesting. Some were "confused," distressed without the teacher telling them what to do, without specific assignments to complete. The majority of the class thought the day was great, but some expressed concern over the noise level and a few students goofing off all day. Most felt that they had accomplished as much work as we usually do, and they enjoyed being able to work at a task until it was completed, without the pressure of a time limit. They liked doing things without being forced to do them, as well as deciding what to do. They begged to continue the experiment, so that's what we decided to do for two more days. We could then reevaluate the plan.

The next morning, I implemented the idea of a "work contract." I gave them ditto sheets listing all our subjects, with suggestions for activities or accomplishments under each. The sheet had a space for their plans in each area and for comments on completion.

Each student was to write a contract for the day, choosing the areas in which to work and planning specifically what to do. After completing an exercise, drill, or review, the student was to check and correct the work, using the teacher's manual. The work was kept in a folder with the contract.

I met individually with the students to discuss their plans. Some had completed theirs quickly, and we discussed as a group what this might mean and what to do about it. One student suggested that a plan might not be challenging enough, that an adjustment should be made, perhaps going on or adding another idea to a day's plan.

I provided resource materials, we discussed suggestions, and I made available drill materials to use when needed. I found I had much more time, so I worked, talked, and spent the time with individuals and groups. At the end of the third day, I evaluated the work folder with each student. To solve the problem of grades, I asked each child to tell me what she had learned.

March 12, Progress Report. Our experiment has, in fact, become our program—with some adjustments. Some children continued to feel frustrated and insecure without teacher direction. Discipline also continued to be a problem with some; and I began to realize that although some children may need the program more than others, I was expecting too much from them too soon—not everyone was ready to assume self-direction yet. Perhaps a gradual weaning from the spoon-fed procedures was necessary.

I regrouped the class, creating two groups. The larger group is the nondirected group. The smaller is teacher-directed, made up of children who want to return to the former teacher-directed method, plus those who, for varied reasons, are unable to function in the self-directed situation. I would have waited longer to see what would happen, but the situation for some disintegrated a little more each day, penalizing the whole class. The disruptions kept everyone upset and limited those who wanted to study and work. So I thought it best for the group as a whole, as well as for the program, to modify the plan.

Those who continued the experiment have forged ahead. I showed them how to design or program their work, using their texts as a basic guide. They have learned that they can teach themselves (and each other) and that I am available when a step is not clear or advice is needed.

At the end of each week, they evaluate themselves in each area in terms of work accomplished, accuracy, and progress toward long-term goals. We learned that the number of errors is not a criterion of failure or success, for errors can and should be part of the learning process. We also discussed that consistently perfect scores may mean that the work is not challenging enough and perhaps we should move on. After self-evaluation, each student brings the evaluation sheet and work folder to discuss with me.

Some of the group members working with me are most anxious to become "independent" students. We evaluate together each week their progress toward that goal. Some students (two or three) who originally wanted to return to the teacher-directed program are now anticipating going back into the self-directed program. (I sense that it has been difficult for them to readjust to the old program.)

Scenario II: Using the Model with Individual Students

John Denbro, a 26-year-old high school English teacher in suburban Chicago, is concerned about Mary Ann Fortnay, one of his students.

Mary Ann is a compulsive worker, who does an excellent job with litera-ture assignments and writes excellent short stories. She is, however, re-luctant to share those stories with other class members and declines to participate in any activities in the performing arts.

Mr. Denbro recognizes that the issue cannot be forced. Mary Ann makes her own decisions about participation that involves sharing her ideas. But he wants her to understand why she is reluctant to allow any public display of her talents.

One afternoon she asks him to read some of her pieces and give her his opinion. Their discussion follows:

Mary Ann. Mr. Denbro, could you take a look at these for me?

Mr. Denbro. Why sure, Mary Ann. Another short story?

Mary Ann. No, some poems I've been working on. I don't think they're very good, but I'd like you to tell me what you think.

Mr. Denbro. When did you write them?

Mary Ann. One Sunday afternoon a couple of weeks ago.

Mr. Denbro. Do you remember what started you thinking that you wanted to write a poem?

Mary Ann. I was feeling kind of sad and I remembered last month when we tried to read "The Waste Land," and it seemed to be trying to say a lot of things that we couldn't say in the usual way. I liked the begin-ning lines, "April is the cruelest month, breeding lilacs out of the dead land" [T.S. Eliot, "The Waste Land"].

Mr. Denbro. And this is what you wrote down?

Mary Ann. Yes. It's the first time I've ever tried writing anything like this.

Mr. Denbro. (Reads for a few minutes, then looks up.) Mary Ann, these are really good.

Mary Ann. What makes a poem good, Mr. Denbro?

Mr. Denbro. Well, there are a variety of ways to judge poetry. Some methods are technical and have to do with the quality of expression and the way one uses metaphor, analogies, and other literary devices. Others are subjective and involve the quality of expression, the real beauty of the words themselves.

Mary Ann. I felt very good when I was writing them, but when I read them over, they sound a little dumb to me.

Mr. Denbro. What do you mean?

Mary Ann. Oh, I don't know. I guess the main thing is that I feel ashamed if anybody else sees them.

Mr. Denbro. Ashamed?

Mary Ann. I really don't know. I just know that if these were to be read aloud, say to my class, I would die of mortification.

Mr. Denbro. You really feel that the class would laugh at these?

Mary Ann. Oh sure, they wouldn't understand.

Mr. Denbro. How about your short stories? How do you feel about them?

Mary Ann. You know I don't want *anybody* to see what I write.

Mr. Denbro. You really feel that you want to put them away somewhere so nobody can see them?

Mary Ann. Yes, I really think so. I don't know exactly why, but I'm pretty sure that no one in my class would understand them.

Mr. Denbro. Can you think of anybody else that might understand them?

Mary Ann. I don't know. I kind of think there are people out there who might, but nobody around here, probably.

Mr. Denbro. How about your parents?

Mary Ann. Oh, they like everything I write.

Mr. Denbro. Well, that makes three of us. Can you think of anybody else?

Mary Ann. I guess I think adults would, but I'm not really so sure about other kids.

Mr. Denbro. Kids are somehow different from adults in this respect?

Mary Ann. Well, kids just don't seem to be interested in these kinds of things. I feel they put down anybody who tries to write anything.

Mr. Denbro. Do you think they feel this way about the authors we read in class?

Mary Ann. Well, sometimes they do, but I guess a lot of the time they really enjoy the stories.

Mr. Denbro. Well then, why do you think they wouldn't like what you write?

Mary Ann. I guess I really don't know, Mr. Denbro. I guess I'm really afraid, but I can't put my finger on it.

Mr. Denbro. Something holds you back.

Mary Ann. In a lot of ways, I really would like to find out whether anybody would appreciate what I write. I just don't know how to go about it.

Mr. Denbro. How would you feel if I were to read one of your short stories but not tell them who wrote it?

Mary Ann. Would you promise?

Mr. Denbro. Of course I would. Then we could talk about how everybody reacted. You would know that they didn't know who had written it.

Mary Ann. I don't know, but it sounds interesting.

Mr. Denbro. Depending on what happened, we could cook up some kind of strategy about what to do next.

Mary Ann. Well, I guess you've got me right where I don't have anything to lose.

Mr. Denbro. I hope we're always where you don't have anything to lose, Mary Ann. But there's always a risk in telling about ourselves.

Mary Ann. What do you mean, "telling about ourselves"?

Mr. Denbro. I have to go now. But let me pick one of your stories and read it next week, and then let's get together on Wednesday and talk about what happened.

Mary Ann. Okay, and you promise not to tell?

Mr. Denbro. I promise. I'll see you next Wednesday after school.

Mary Ann. Okay. Thanks a lot, Mr. Denbro. Have a good weekend.

Commentary on Scenarios

Both Karla Trobaugh and John Denbro were using the nondirective teaching model based on the work of psychologist and counselor Carl Rogers (1982) and other advocates of nondirective counseling. Rogers believed that positive human relationships enable people to grow; therefore, instruction should be based on concepts of human relations in contrast to concepts of subject matter. Basically, he extended to education his view of therapy as a mode of learning.

For three decades, Rogers (1961, 1982) has been the acknowledged spokesperson for models in which the teacher plays the role of counselor. Developed from counseling theory, the model emphasizes a partnership between students and teacher. The role of the teacher is primarily facilitative: to help students understand how to have a major part in directing their own educations—for example, by encouraging behavior that clarifies goals and motivates students to participate in developing avenues for reaching those goals; to provide information on the progress students are making; to help as needed as students try to work out their problems; and to actively build the partnerships required.

PURPOSES AND ATTRIBUTES OF THE PERSONAL MODELS

Personal models of teaching share three purposes:

• To lead students toward greater mental and emotional health by helping them develop self-confidence, form a realistic sense of self, and build empathetic reactions to others.

• To increase the proportion of education that emanates from the needs and aspirations of the student—that is, taking each student as a partner in determining what and how that student will learn.

• To develop specific kinds of qualitative thinking, such as creativity and personal expression.

These models foster growth in the personal domain in at least four ways. First, the models can be used as general models of education. They were used in designing schools where faculties adopted a nondirective philosophy as the core approach to education (e.g., Aspy and Roebuck 1973, Neill 1960) or as a major component (Chamberlin and Chamberlin 1943).

Second, they can be used to flavor a learning environment designed around other models. For example, we can carry around with us concern for students' self-concepts; and we can think carefully about how to shape our lessons, classroom activities, and questions/responses to students to maximize their positive feelings about self and to minimize the likelihood that our teaching will diminish them as people. In other words, we can use these models to attend to our students' personal qualities and feelings and to look for opportunities that make them partners with us.

Third, we can use the unique properties of these models to counsel students when we wish to help them reach out to the world more fully and positively.

Fourth, we can build curriculums in the academic subjects around the models. For example, the "language experience" methods for teaching reading use student-dictated stories as the initial reading materials and student-selected literature as the chief materials once initial competence has been established. Combined with other models, the personal models can be used to design independent-study courses, including resource-based programs.

Over the years, the personal models of teaching have been used with all types of students and across all subjects and teaching roles. Although they are designed to promote self-understanding and independence, they have fared well as a contributor to a wide range of academic objectives (see Aspy and Roebuck 1973, Chamberlin and Chamberlin 1943).

Even though enhancing the learner as a person is a worthwhile educational goal, a major thesis of the personal family of models is that better-developed, more affirmative, self-actualizing learners have increased learning capabilities. This thesis is supported by studies indicating that teachers who incorporate personal models into their repertoires increased achievement among their students (Roebuck, Buhler, and Aspy 1976).

The Behavioral Systems Family

This is a lot better than turning a real chopper upside down.

—ARMY INSTRUCTOR TO BRUCE JOYCE
JUNE 1953

SCENARIO I

Driver education students in a secondary school in Chicago are taking turns in a driving simulator. As the motion picture camera projects an image of the roadway ahead, obstacles appear. A child steps out from behind two parked cars; the "driver" turns the wheel and misses the child. A stop sign appears suddenly beyond a parked truck; the driver slams on the brakes. The driver makes a turn, and a roadway narrows suddenly; again the driver brakes. One by one, the students experience driving under simulated conditions. As students complete the driving course, the instructor and the other students debrief them, questioning their reactions and defensive driving.

SCENARIO II

In another high school classroom, this time in the Boston suburbs, a class is watching a television show. The actors are portraying members of the U.S. cabinet facing a crisis. After examining the issues, the class reaches a conclusion. One student reaches for the telephone in the classroom, dials a number, and speaks to the actors in the studio, suggesting how they might play their roles differently to resolve the crisis. Students in 25 other classrooms are also watching the portrayal and simultaneously debating the issues seen on the television. They, too, are communicating their views to the actors in the studio. The next day, the show resumes. In various ways, the actors play out the suggestions the classes make, and the other members of the cabinet react. Students see not only their ideas brought to life on the television screen but also the consequences of their recommendations.

SCENARIO III

In an inner-city neighborhood in Toronto, an elementary school class is also watching a television screen. The scene portrays a program announcer counting down as a spaceship attempts but fails to break free from the moon's gravity. Class members then take the roles of spaceship crew members. Instructions from the Royal Canadian Space Administration divide them into teams, and they prepare to work together to conserve their life-support systems and to manage their relationships in the spaceship until repairs can be made.

SCENARIO IV

In San Antonio, two groups of middle school students enter a room. One group represents the alpha culture; the other, the beta culture. Their task is to learn how to communicate with others who have learned rules and patterns of behavior from a different society. Gradually, they learn to master communication patterns. Simultaneously, they become aware that as members of a culture, they have inherited powerful patterns that strongly influence their personalities and ways of communicating with others.

SCENARIO V

In Livingston, Montana, a 5th grade class is engaged in a caribou hunt, using a computer simulation. As they progress through the hunt, modeled on behaviors of the Netsilik Eskimos, they learn behavior patterns of the Netsilik and begin to compare those patterns with the ones they use in their everyday lives.

SCENARIO VI

In Statesboro, Georgia, a group of high school seniors faces a hypothetical problem posed by the U.S. secretary of state. Agronomists have developed a nutrient that when added to the food of beef cattle greatly increases their weight. Only a limited amount of this nutrient is available, and the students must determine how the nutrient will be divided among the needy nations of the world. Congress has imposed the following restraints: Recipient nations must have a reasonable supply of beef cattle, must not be aligned with the hard-core Communist bloc of nations, must not be vegetarians, and must have a population that exceeds a certain size.

The students debate the alternatives. Some countries are ruled out immediately. Of the remaining countries, some seem attractive at first, yet less attractive later. The students grapple with the problems of humanity and ideology and with practical situations. In this simulation, they face the problems of the committees of scientists who continually advise the U.S. government on various courses of action.

SCENARIO VII

In the quiet of our homes, Carmen San Diego's gang of thieves takes our children to explore the world.

RESEARCH

Of the four families we explore, the behavioral systems family, which is based on the work of B.F. Skinner and the cybernetic training psychologists (Smith and Smith 1966), has the most literature. Studies range from programmed instruction to simulations and include training models (Joyce and Showers 1983) and methods derived directly from therapy (Wolpe and Lazarus 1966).

There is a great deal of research on the application of social learning theory to instruction (Becker and Gersten 1982), training (Smith and Smith 1966), and simulations (Boocock and Schild 1968). Behavioral technologists have demonstrated that they can design programs for both specific and general goals (Becker and Gersten 1982) and have shown that the effective application of those techniques requires extensive cognitive activity and precise interactive skills (Spaulding 1970).

An analysis by White (1978) examines the results of studies on the application of the DISTAR version of social learning theory to special education. The average effect sizes for mathematics and reading range from about one-half to one standard deviation. The effects for moderately and severely handicapped students are similar. Perhaps most important, a few studies include the effects on aptitude (measures of intellectual ability), and when the DISTAR program was implemented for several years, the effect sizes are 1.0 or above, representing an increase of about 10 points in the standard IQ ratio.

Thoresen and Mahoney (1974) concentrated on teaching people to change their behavior by developing their own programs. Some of the most interesting work relates to the self-curing of phobias, such as acrophobia, and teaching people to monitor and modify their behavior in social situations, such as overcoming excessive shyness and aggressiveness.

THE SIMULATION MODEL AS AN ILLUSTRATION

From the various behavioral/cybernetic models, we selected simulation as our illustrative model for the behavioral systems family. This section briefly explores the principles of simulation, discusses various types of simulations, and explains the model's orientation. Simulations are built using cybernetic principles that emphasize the self-correcting dimension of behavioral theory. Briefly, as we behave, observe the consequences of our behavior, and decide if the consequences represent "success" or progress toward a goal, we modify our behavior.

Principles of Simulation

The seven scenarios earlier in this chapter describe simulations. Elements of the real world were simplified and presented in a form that can be contained inside a classroom, workroom, or living room. The attempt is to approximate realistic conditions so that the concepts learned and problem-solutions generated are transferrable to the real world and to understanding and performing tasks related to the content of the simulation.

Most simulations are constructed from descriptions of real-life situations, and a less-than-real-life environment is created for the instructional situation. Sometimes, the renditions are quite elaborate (e.g., flight and space flight simulators or simulations of international relations). Students engage in an activity to achieve the goal of the simulation (e.g., to get an aircraft off the ground or to redevelop an urban area) and deal with realistic factors until the goal is mastered.

To progress through the simulation tasks, students must develop concepts and skills necessary to perform in the specified area. In some of the simulations described earlier, the drivers had to develop concepts and skills for driving effectively; the caribou hunters had to learn concepts about a certain culture; and the cabinet members had to learn about international relations and the problems of governing a nation.

Students also learn from the consequences of their actions. A driver who does not turn rapidly enough "hits" the child she is trying to avoid; she must learn to turn more quickly. Yet if the car turns too quickly, it goes out of control and veers to the other side of the street. The driver has to learn to correct the initial move while keeping her eyes on the road and looking for yet other obstacles. Students who do poorly in the caribou hunt learn what happens if the culture does not function efficiently or if its members shrink from carrying out the tasks that enable them to survive.

Types of Simulations

Some simulations are games; some are not. Some are competitive; some are cooperative. And some are played by individuals against their own standard. For example, competition is important in the familiar board game Monopoly, which simulates the activity of real estate speculators and incorporates many elements of real-life speculation. Players learn the rules of investment and speculation as embodied in the game.

In simulations such as the Life Career game, players attempt to reach their goals noncompetitively. No score is kept, but interactions are recorded and analyzed later. Students play out the life cycle of a human being: They select mates; choose careers; decide whether to obtain various amounts of education; and learn, through the consequences of their decisions, how these choices can affect their lives.

In computer simulations like Sim City and Sim Earth, students can play alone or together against their own standard for creating a good quality of life.

Nearly all simulations depend on print—materials and various paraphernalia—from the driving simulator, to the information and materials about the life of Netsilik Eskimos, to the Monopoly board (money and symbols of property), to the computer and software program of Sim Earth.

Effective classroom use of the simulation model depends on a teacher's blending the already prepared simulation into a curriculum, highlighting and reinforcing the learning inherent in the program. The teacher's ability to make the activities meaningful is critical. That said, however, the self-instructional property of simulations is vital.

Orientation to the Model

Simulations have increasingly been used in education over the last 30 years, but the simulation model did not originate within the field of education. Rather, it is an application of the principles of cybernetics, a branch of psychology. Making an analogy between humans and machines, cybernetic psychologists conceptualize the learner as a self-regulating feedback system. The central focus is the apparent similarity between the feedback control mechanisms of electromechanical systems and human systems.

"A feedback control system incorporates three primary functions: It generates movement of the system toward a target or defined path; it compares the effects of this action with the true path and detects error; and it utilizes this error signal to redirect the system" (Smith and Smith 1966, p. 203). For example, the automatic pilot of a ship continually corrects the helm, depending on compass readings. When the ship begins to swing in a certain direction and the compass moves off the desired heading more than a certain amount, a motor is switched on and the helm moves over. When the ship returns to its course, the helm straightens out again, and the ship continues on its way. The automatic pilot operates in essentially the same way as a human pilot does. Both watch the compass, and both move the wheel to the left or right, depending on what is going on. Both initiate action in terms of a specified goal (e.g., "Let's go north"), and depending on the feedback or error signal, both redirect the initial action. Complex self-regulating mechanical systems have been developed to control devices such as guided missiles, ocean liners, and satellites.

Cybernetic psychologists interpret the human being as a control system that generates a course of action and then redirects or corrects the action using feedback. This can be a complicated process—such as when the secretary of state reevaluates foreign policy. Or it can be a simple one—such as when we notice that our sailboat is heading into the wind too much and we ease off on our course just a little. In using mechanical systems as a frame of reference for analyzing human beings, psychologists came up with the central idea "that performance and learning must be analyzed in terms of the control relationships between a human operator and an instrumental situation." That is, learning was understood to be determined by the nature of the individual, as well as by the design of the learning situation (Smith and Smith 1966, p. vii).

According to cybernetic psychology, all human behavior involves a perceptible pattern of motion. This pattern includes both covert behavior, such as thinking and symbolic behavior, and overt behavior. In any given situation, individuals modify their behavior according to the feedback they receive from the environment. They organize their movements and response patterns in relation to this feedback. Thus, their own sensorimotor capabilities form the basis of their feedback systems. This ability to receive feedback constitutes the human system's mechanism for receiving and sending information. As human beings develop greater linguistic capability, they are able to use indirect as well as direct feedback, thereby expanding their control over the physical and social environment. That is, they are less dependent on the concrete realities of the environment because they can use its symbolic representations.

The essence, then, of cybernetic psychology is the principle of sense-oriented feedback that is intrinsic to an individual (one "feels" the effects of one's decisions) and is the basis for self-corrective choices. For example, in the driving simulation, if the driver heads into curves too rapidly and then has to jerk the wheel to avoid going off the road, this feedback permits the driver to adjust his behavior so that when driving on a real road, he will turn more gingerly when approaching sharp curves. A cybernetic psychologist designs simulators so that the feedback about the consequences of behavior enables learners to modify their responses and develop a repertoire of appropriate behaviors.

Individuals can feel the effects of their decisions because the environment responds *in full*, rather than simply, "You're right!" or "Wrong! Try again." The environmental consequences of their choices are played back to them. *Learning*, in cybernetic terms, is sensorially experiencing the environmental consequences of one's behavior and engaging in self-corrective behavior. *Instruction*, in cybernetic terms, is designed to create an environment for the learner in which this full feedback takes place.

FROM THE BEHAVIORAL STANCE: TIPS FOR TEACHERS

Although we concentrated primarily on simulation, which is only one model from the behavioral systems family, the frame of reference of behavioral psychologists can be used to think about many common classroom events. Here are some examples in the form of questions and tips.

Classroom Rules

Which is better, a list of behaviors to avoid and negative reinforcers (e.g., "A one-time violation results in your name on the board, a two-time violation results in loss of recess, . . .") or a list of desirable behaviors and rewards (e.g., a certificate proclaiming, "You are a Super Student!" "You are a Great Reader")?

Tip: The higher-probability bet is the positive rules and positive reinforcers or nurturers.

Off-Task Behavior

If 28 students are on task and two are off task, which teacher behavior has the higher probability of succeeding in bringing the two into an on-task mode: reprimanding the off-task students or praising the on-task students?

Tip: Praising the on-task students is better (positive rather than negative reinforcement).

Instruction or Self-Instruction

In the computer lab, when introducing a new word processing program to students who can already use another program, one teacher takes the students step-by-step through the manual. The other teacher gives the students the program and, after a brief orientation, asks them to teach themselves to use the program. Which works better?

Tip: Controlling your own learning schedule arouses positive affect. Also, pacing is under the control of the individual, who can move rapidly or slowly according to individual needs.

Itchy Students

A kid just doesn't seem to sit still or pay attention for more than a few minutes at a time. Do you: Give the kid extra homework when she wanders off task, or teach her how to use a relaxation exercise when the hyperactive feeling rises?

Tip: The first choice is a negative reinforcer that also uses academic work as a punishment, which can produce an aversive response to academic tasks and assignments in general. The second provides effective control, makes the student a partner in regulating her behavior, and provides the opportunity for positive self-reinforcement as well as external reinforcement.

Motivation

Following a test at the end of a mathematics unit, one teacher asks students to correct their own papers and figure out their gain scores. The other teacher scores the tests and provides the students with an analysis of items missed. Which is the better bet for motivating the students?

Tip: Self-scoring, emphasis on progress, and setting of new goals work almost every time.

Expanding the Teaching Repertoire

Inquiry into teaching and learning makes the life of educators. They create environments, study how students respond, and watch them learn how to learn. We believe that reflection on teaching can be greatly enhanced through the study of teaching strategies that have been submitted to intense scrutiny and development. Practice, theory, and research become intertwined, and the body of professional knowledge becomes enhanced as each of us generates information about student learning.

In this chapter, we consider how educators working as individuals, as a faculty, and within teaching centers can enhance their repertoire of teaching models. We have research to help us. Studies of teachers who are learning the teaching models indicate that three learning processes mingle together in the progression of adding to a teacher's repertoire:

• Developing an understanding of a model: how and why it works and how it can be modulated to take individual differences into account. Such learning involves lots of reading and discussion—getting hold of the books and articles that describe the model and its rationale and analyzing them thoroughly.

• Forming a picture of the model in action: envisioning what the teacher does and what students do and how the instructional and social environments are managed in the model. This learning requires watching and analyzing demonstrations so that the process becomes clear. A teacher begins to "feel" the model in action and sense how to teach the students to use it as a tool for learning. Our rule of thumb is that one has to see a new model about 20 times to get that feel.

• Adapting the model to what a teacher teaches—to the goals of the parts of the curriculum for which the teacher is responsible. After adapting the model, the teacher practices until executive control over the model is achieved. Forty or 50 hours of classroom practice are needed, plus the preparation time for that many hours of instruction.

Optimally, these three learning processes are mixed. A teacher reads, watches, reads some more, watches and practices, reads and watches and practices, and so on.

WORKING INDIVIDUALLY

Suppose that you (e.g., a principal, teacher, staff developer, or curriculum consultant) decide to study models of teaching and have no colleague willing to join you. (If someone is available, enlist that person immediately, because it will make the process much easier!) No matter, you can do it yourself. You just have to figure out how to manage the three processes of learning while working alone. Here are some of our tested suggestions:

1. Study one model at a time until you have mastered it.

2. Read anything you can find that is pertinent to the model. *Models of Teaching* (Joyce and Weil 1996) is a handy guide to the literature.

3. Try to find a workshop conducted by an expert in using the model. Make sure the workshop includes lots of demonstrations. If you can't find a workshop, then obtain videotapes of the model in action and study them. Watching a few tapes again and again is a big help.

4. Practice like crazy. Prepare short lessons and long units—both are necessary. After a few practices with your students, read some more, watch the tapes again, then practice. Make sure your practice is regular—don't let long periods go by between them—and that the practice is within your normal content area, where you have the greatest substantive control.

You'll feel uncomfortable at first. Ignore the discomfort and keep practicing. After a few tries, you will begin to get the feel of the moves of the model, and the adaptation to your curriculum areas will become easier. Be sure to study what the students are learning, both about substance and about how to learn.

WORKING AS A FACULTY

Suppose that you are working with a faculty that is studying teaching strategies. We suggest the following approach:

1. Organize peer coaching groups. Form partners within the faculty—no more than one or two people—who can work together to study the new teaching strategies. Develop a weekly schedule for peer coaching—about an hour each week—when the teams can meet, preferably in the same setting at the same time, to share plans and progress.

2. Plan to study one model at a time; arrangements to do only one are difficult enough.

3. Proceed, using the suggestions for working individually: Study the literature of the model, watch demonstrations, and practice. The difference is that now you have the companionship of others as you work toward effective implementation. Thus, you can exploit some dimensions of the model more rapidly and powerfully. For example, you can have a cumulative impact on students throughout the school when all students are taught a model of learning. In addition, the entire faculty can study the effects on student learning.

Consider as an example of faculty efforts a study undertaken by the Kaiser School faculty. The teachers at Kaiser Elementary School in the Newport/Costa Mesa School District, California, have been learning to use the inductive thinking model of teaching to help their students connect reading and writing. The objective is to see if the students can learn to generate better quality writing by analyzing how expert writers work. For example, when studying how to introduce characters, students classify the approaches authors use in the books they are reading, then experiment with the devices they have identified.

Periodically, teachers ask students to produce writing elicited with standardized content and prompts. For example, students watch a film segment that introduces a character and then provide a written introduction to the character. The samples of writing are scored with an instrument that was developed at the UCLA Center for Research on

Evaluation (Quellmalz and Burry 1983) to measure quality of writing across the grades and that yields scores on three dimensions of quality.

The year before the teachers began to study the teaching of writing using the inductive thinking model, the average student gain in writing quality during a year was about 20 points on the scale. For example, the grade 4 average score rose from 180 to 200; the grade 6 average score rose from 220 to 240. As teachers taught students to make the connection between reading and writing, the average gain jumped to 90 points the first year. The average student gained about four and a half times more than the average gain the previous year. No student gained less than 40 points, and some gained as much as 140 points.

The Kaiser teachers surveyed the research on the teaching of writing and found some examples of what looked like large gains when particular curriculum approaches were implemented. They wondered how they could compare the results of their efforts when some of the studies used different scales.

When the Kaiser School faculty discovered the concept of effect size (see Appendix for an explanation of "effect size"), they were able to calculate the effects of their efforts in such a way that they could compare their results to those of other efforts. They consulted the review of research on writing conducted by George Hillocks (1987) and found that the average effect size of "inquiry" approaches to the teaching of writing was 0.67 compared to textbook-oriented instruction. The average student in the inquiry treatment was at about the 70th percentile of the distributions of students taught by the textbook method.

The teachers carefully calculated the effect size for each grade. For example, when the inductive thinking model was used in the 1994–95 school year, the 6th grade gained an average of 90 points, compared with an average gain of 20 points in the 1993–94 school year (the control), a difference of 70 points. The standard deviation of the control year was 55. Dividing 55 into 70, they calculated an effect size of 1.27, nearly twice the average in the Hillocks review. The average student in the first year of using the inductive thinking model was at approximately the 90th percentile of the distribution for the control year. Figure 7.1 (see p. 69) depicts the two distributions.

The Kaiser teachers are inquirers. They conduct individual and schoolwide action research. They selected a model of teaching, studied it, learned how to use it, and inquired into its effects on their students. Their collective inquiry and its results on student learning will lead them to search for ways of using that model across curriculum areas and to look for and create other models that can serve their students. They are classic teacher-researchers.

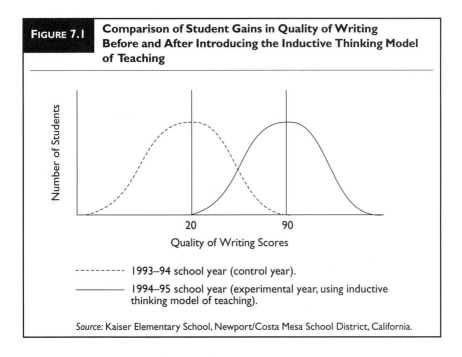

FIGURE 7.1

Comparison of Student Gains in Quality of Writing Before and After Introducing the Inductive Thinking Model of Teaching

Number of Students

20   90

Quality of Writing Scores

- - - - - - - 1993–94 school year (control year).

—————— 1994–95 school year (experimental year, using inductive thinking model of teaching).

Source: Kaiser Elementary School, Newport/Costa Mesa School District, California.

WORKING WITHIN A TEACHING CENTER

Now, suppose that you are responsible for the organization of a teaching center sponsored by a school district or intermediate agency. Part of your job is to support school-based improvement and help educators study, generate, and use alternative models of teaching.

Similar to working individually or as part of a faculty group, you need to provide the conditions that permit people to learn about the teaching strategies: They need opportunities to study the literature; watch demonstrations; and practice, with support preferably from peer coaching teams. Thus, your workshops need to contain the elements that support those conditions.

Your offerings can be for individuals, groups (better), entire faculties (even better), or the faculty of an entire district (can work very well). Participants will need some guidance:

• They need to be organized into peer coaching teams, and time should be provided for them to meet and study together.

• They need help learning how to study student learning in an action research framework.

• They need to study implementation and effects on students so that they can assess the results of their efforts.

An example of a teaching center effort is the Richmond Program, conducted by organizers of the Richmond County, Georgia, School Improvement Program (see Joyce et al. 1996). From the beginning, the intention of the Richmond Program was to increase the capacity of the school district as a unit to sustain and expand school improvement initiatives, thus reducing and then eliminating the need for external support. A primary means for increasing local capacity was the development of a community of teachers and administrators who could carry forth all phases of the initiative, introducing more schools to the processes (outlined earlier), providing staff development on models of teaching, supporting study groups and building leadership teams, and giving help to other groups of schools.

The cadre was recruited from the pool of teachers who had made outstanding progress with models of teaching and who showed leadership in their schools in study groups and schoolwide organization. Those wishing to be candidates for the cadre submitted videotapes of how they used each model in the classroom. The selection team visited the candidates in their classrooms, watching them teach and interviewing them.

An initial cadre of 20 persons was organized to receive additional training beyond that provided to other district teachers and administrators. The training included how to organize faculties and study groups and how to conduct training and study implementation.

The Richmond cadre of teachers disseminated the teaching strategies to other schools in the district. Results in the first nine schools (16 were eventually involved) on the Iowa Tests of Basic Skills battery were substantial. Each of the nine schools completed eight tests for a total of 72 test scores. Forty of the 72 scores reflected gains of greater than four months over the previous year's results, and 20 of the 72 scores reflected gains of two and four months.

Studying teaching pays off! We have a knowledge base that can help individuals, faculties, and entire districts or regions expand the teaching and learning opportunities available to students. All it takes to get started is the willingness to inquire into this knowledge base, to inquire into our practice, and to inquire more fully into what and how students learn.

Appendix:
The Concept of Effect Size

We use the concept of "effect size" (Glass 1982) to describe the magnitude of gains from any given change in educational practice and thus to predict what we can hope to accomplish by using that practice. To introduce the concept, let us consider a study conducted by Dr. Bharati Baveja (1988) with one of the authors in the Motilal Nehru School of Sports, about 30 miles northwest of New Delhi, India. Dr. Baveja designed her study to test the effectiveness of using an inductive thinking approach to teach a botany unit, compared with using an intensive tutorial treatment. Before instruction began, all the students took a test to assess their knowledge and divided into two groups of equal ability. The control group studied the material with the aid of tutoring and lectures—standard treatment in Indian schools for courses of this type. The experimental group worked in pairs and were led through inductive and concept attainment exercises emphasizing classification of plants.

Figure A.1 (see p. 73) shows the distribution of scores for the experimental and control groups on the post-test, which like the pre-test, contained items dealing with information on the unit.

The difference between the experimental and control groups was a little above a standard deviation. The difference, computed in terms of standard deviations, is the *effect size of the inductive thinking treatment*. What that means is that the experimental group mean (average) score was where the 80th percentile score was for the control group. The dif-

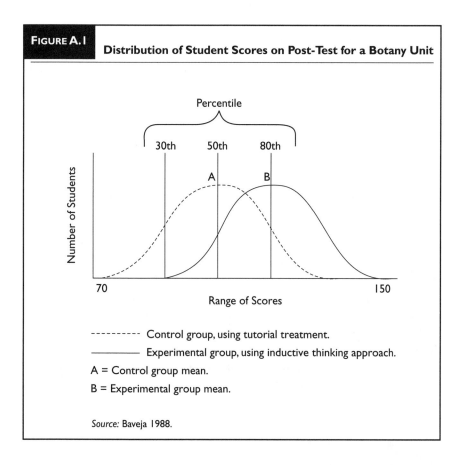

FIGURE A.1

Distribution of Student Scores on Post-Test for a Botany Unit

Percentile

30th   50th   80th

A   B

Number of Students

70   150

Range of Scores

-------- Control group, using tutorial treatment.

———— Experimental group, using inductive thinking approach.

A = Control group mean.

B = Experimental group mean.

Source: Baveja 1988.

ference increased when a delayed recall test was given 10 months later, indicating that the information acquired with the concept-oriented strategies was retained somewhat better than information gained using the control treatment.

Calculations like these enable us to compare the magnitude of the potential effects of the innovations (e.g., teaching skills and strategies, curriculums, and technologies) that we might use in an effort to affect student learning. We can also determine whether the treatment has different effects for all kinds of students or just for some. In the Baveja study, the experimental treatment was apparently effective for the whole population. The lowest score in the experimental group distribution was about where the 30th percentile score was for the control group, and about 30 percent of the students in the experimental group exceeded the highest score obtained in the control group.

Although substantial in its own right, learning and retention of information was modest when we consider the effect on the students' ability to identify plants and their characteristics, which was measured on a separate test. The scores for students from the experimental group were *eight* times higher than the scores for the control group. Dr. Baveja's inquiry confirmed her hypothesis that the students using the inductive thinking model were able to apply the information and concepts from the unit much more effectively than were the students from the tutorial treatment.

To deepen our understanding, let's work through some concepts that are useful. We describe distributions of scores in terms of the *central tendencies,* which refer to the clustering of scores around the middle of the distribution, and *variance,* or their dispersion. Concepts describing central tendency include the *average* or arithmetic *mean,* the sum of the scores divided by the number of scores; the *median* or middle score (half of the scores are above, and half are below the median score); and the *mode,* which is the most frequent score (graphically, the highest point in the distribution). In Figure A.2, the average, the median, and the mode are in the same place because the distribution is symmetrical.

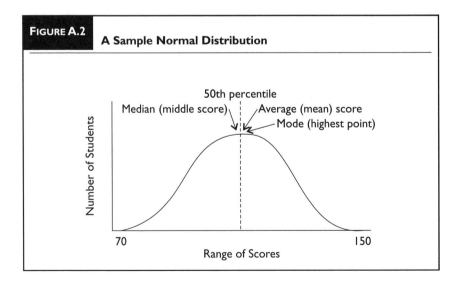

FIGURE A.2   **A Sample Normal Distribution**

Dispersion of a distribution is described in terms of *range, rank,* and *standard deviation:*

• *Range.* The distance between the highest and lowest scores (see Figure A.2).

• *Rank.* Frequently described in percentile. For example, the 20th score from the top in a 100-person distribution is at the 80th percentile, because 20 percent of the scores are above and 80 percent are below it.

• *Standard Deviation.* Describes how widely or narrowly scores are distributed. In Figure A.2, the range is 70 (lowest score) to 150 (highest score). The 50th percentile score is at the middle (in this case, corresponding with the average, the mode, and the median). In Figure A.3, the standard deviations are marked off by vertical lines labeled –2 SD, –1 SD, +1 SD, +2 SD, and +3 SD. Note that the percentile rank of the score one standard deviation above the mean (+1 SD) is 84 (84 percent of the scores are below that point); the rank two standard deviations above the mean (+2 SD) is 97; and three standard deviations above the mean is 99.

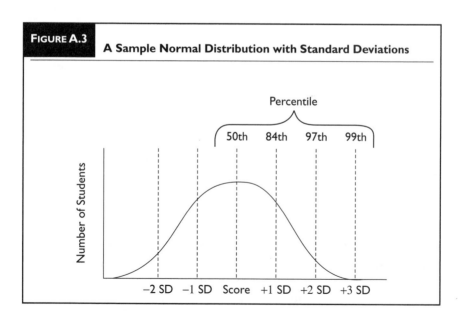

FIGURE A.3   **A Sample Normal Distribution with Standard Deviations**

When the mean, median, and mode coincide, as in this distribution, and the distribution of scores is as symmetrical as those in Figure A.2 and Figure A.3, the distribution is referred to as *normal.* This concept is useful in statistical operations, although many actual distributions are not symmetrical.

To explain the concept of effect size, we will use symmetrical, or "normal," distributions. Thus, in Figure A.4 (see p. 77), we convert the results of the study of group investigation that appears in Figure 4.1 (Sharan and Shachar 1988) to graphical form. Figure A.4 compares the post-test scores of the low SES students in the group investigation and whole class treatments. The average score of the group investigation treatment (50.17) corresponds to about the 92nd percentile of the distribution of the whole class students. The effect size is computed by dividing the difference between the two means by the standard deviation of the whole class (control) group. The effect size in this case is 1.6 standard deviations, using the formula

$$ES = \frac{\text{average of experimental group} - \text{average of control group}}{\text{standard deviation of control group}}$$

$$\frac{50.17 - 27.23}{13.73} = 1.6$$

Figures like Figure A.4 provide an idea about the relative effects one can expect if one teaches students with each model of teaching compared with using the normative patterns of curriculum and instruction. We create each figure from an analysis of the research base that is currently available, and we can usually build the figure to depict the average effects from large numbers of studies.

When studying the research base to decide when to use a given model of teaching, it is important to realize that size of effects is not the only consideration. We also have to consider the nature of the objectives and the uses of the model. For example, in Spaulding's (1970) study, the effect size on ability measures was just 0.5, or about a half standard deviation (see Figure A.5 on p. 78).

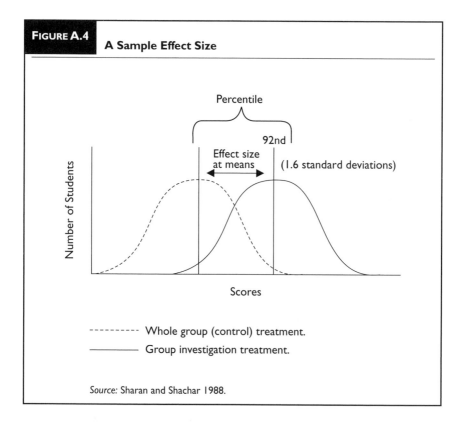

FIGURE A.4

A Sample Effect Size

Percentile

92nd

Effect size at means   (1.6 standard deviations)

Number of Students

Scores

- - - - - - - - - Whole group (control) treatment.
——————— Group investigation treatment.

Source: Sharan and Shachar 1988.

Ability, however, is a powerful attribute, and a model or combination of models that can increase ability affects everything the student does for years to come, increasing learning through those years. The simplest cooperative learning procedures have relatively modest effect sizes. These procedures affect not only feelings about self as a learner but also social skills and academic learning. In addition, they are easy to use and have wide applications. Thus, their modest effect can be felt more regularly and broadly than some models that have more dramatic effect sizes with respect to a given objective.

Some models can help us almost eliminate dispersion in a distribution. For example, a colleague used mnemonic devices to teach his 4th grade students the names of the states and their capitals. *All* his students learned all of them—and remembered them throughout the year.

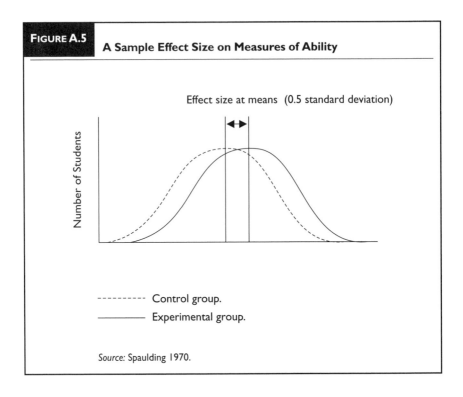

FIGURE A.5   A Sample Effect Size on Measures of Ability

Effect size at means (0.5 standard deviation)

Number of Students

--------- Control group.
————— Experimental group.

Source: Spaulding 1970.

Thus, the distribution of his class's scores on tests of their ability to supply all the names on a blank map had no range. The average score was the top possible score. There were no percentile ranks because the students' scores were all tied at the top. For some objectives—for example, basic knowledge about the U.S. Constitution, computation skills, and a basic reading vocabulary—we want, in fact, to have a high degree of success for all our students because anything less disadvantages them—and society.

Although high effect sizes make a treatment attractive, size alone is not the only consideration when choosing among alternatives. Modest effect sizes that affect many people can have a large payoff for the population. An example from medicine is helpful. Suppose a dread disease is affecting a population and we possess a vaccine that will reduce the chances of contracting the disease by only 10 percent. If one million persons might become infected without the vaccine but 900,000 might become infected if it is used, the modest effect of the vaccine might save 100,000 lives.

In education, some estimates suggest that during the first year of school, about one million children yearly (30 percent) make little progress toward learning to read. We also know that lack of success in reading instruction is a dread educational disease, because for each year that initial instruction is unsuccessful, the probability that the student will respond to instruction later is greatly lowered. Would a modestly effective treatment, say one that reduced the lack of success in the first year for 50,000 children (5 percent), be worthwhile? We think so. Also, several such treatments might be cumulative. Of course, we prefer a high-effect treatment, but one is not always available. Even when it is, it might not reach some students, and we might need to resort to a less powerful choice for those students.

Also, different types of effects need to be considered, such as attitudes, values, concepts, intellectual development, skills, and information. Using the preceding example of early reading, two treatments may be approximately equal in terms of learning to read in the short run, but one treatment may affect attitudes positively and leave the students feeling confident and ready to try again. Similarly, two social studies programs may achieve similar amounts of information and concepts, but one might excel in attitudes toward citizenship. In the most dramatic instances, when the effect size reaches five or six standard deviations, the lowest-scoring student in the experimental treatment exceeds the highest-scoring student in the control treatment! This is a rare event, of course, but when it does occur, it gives us great hope about the potential of educational practice.

Again, as we study some practices and the effects that can be expected from them, we should not concentrate on magnitude of effects alone. Self-instruction programs that are as effective as standard instruction can be useful because they enable students to teach themselves and can be blended with agent-delivered instruction. Broadcast television, because of its potential to reach many children, can make a big difference even though it is modestly effective in comparison with standard instruction. *Sesame Street* and the *Electric Company* (Ball and Bogatz 1970) are examples. They are not dramatically more effective than 1st grade instruction without them, but they produce positive attitudes and augment instruction handsomely, enabling a certain percentage of students to virtually teach themselves. In fact, distance education and media-based instruction (e.g., learning from television, computer-assisted instruction, and packages of multimedia materials) need not be more effective to be useful. For example, in a high school that does not offer a given foreign language, a student who can learn that language by self-study assisted by such aids as television and computer programs can benefit greatly. The British Open University, operated as distance education augmented by tutorial centers, virtually doubled the number of university graduates in the United Kingdom, and the performance of its students on academic tests compared favorably with the performance of "regular" university students.

Some procedures can interact productively with others. One-to-one tutoring has a large effect size (Bloom 1984) and might interact productively with some teaching strategies. Or, as is evidently the case within the "Success for All" (Slavin and Madden 1995) and "Reading Recovery" (Pinnell 1989) programs, such tutoring is incorporated into a curriculum-management system that enables short periods of tutoring to pay off. On the other hand, tracking hurts the effectiveness of any procedure (Oakes 1986).

Simply learning the size of effects of a year's instruction can be informative, as we learned from the National Assessment of Writing Progress (Applebee, Langer, Jenkins, Mullis, and Foertsch 1990), which discovered that the effect size of instruction in writing nationally is such that the average 8th grade student is about at the 62nd percentile of the 4th grade distribution! Schools may want to learn how much better they can do than that!

There are many kinds of learning measures:

• School grades.
• Measures of conduct, such as counts of referrals and suspensions.
• Simple measures, such as how many books students read.
• Content analyses of student work.
• Study of quality of writing.
• Curriculum-relevant tests (those that measure the content of a unit or course).
• Traditional standardized tests, which can be submitted to an analysis that produces estimates of effect size.

The state of the art is such that any specific curricular or instructional models cannot solve *all* problems of student learning. Educational research is in its infancy. We hope that the readers of this book will not just use it as a source of teaching and learning strategies, but will also learn how to add to the knowledge base. There are more than two million teachers in the United States alone. If only 1 percent conducted and reported one study each year, there would be 20,000 new studies every year, a knowledge increment several times larger than the entire current base. But in addition to contributing to the larger knowledge base, teachers in any school can, by studying their teaching, share ideas that help everyone in the school become more effective.

References

Applebee, A., J. Langer, L. Jenkins, I. Mullis, and M. Foertsch. (1990). *Learning to Write in Our Nation's Schools*. Washington, D.C.: U.S. Department of Education.

Aspy, D.N., and F. Roebuck. (1973). "An Investigation of the Relationship Between Student Levels of Cognitive Functioning and the Teacher's Classroom Behavior." *Journal of Educational Research* 65, 6: 365–368.

Ball, S., and G.A. Bogatz. (1970). *The First Year of Sesame Street*. Princeton, N.J.: Educational Testing Service.

Baveja, B. (1988). *An Exploratory Study of the Use of Information-Processing Models of Teaching in Secondary School Biology Science Classes*. Ph.D. Thesis, Delhi University, Delhi, India.

Becker, W., and R. Gersten. (1982). "A Followup of Follow Through: The Later Effects of the Direct Instruction Model on Children in the Fifth and Sixth Grades." *American Educational Research Journal* 19, 1: 75–92.

Bloom, B.S. (1984). "The 2 Sigma Problem: The Search for Group Instruction as Effective as One-to-One Tutoring." *Educational Researcher* 13, 6: 4–16.

Bonsangue, M.V. (1993). "Long-Term Effects of the Calculus Workshop Model." *Cooperative Learning* 13, 3: 19–20.

Boocock, S.S., and E. Schild. (1968). *Simulation Games in Learning*. Beverly Hills: Sage Publications, Inc.

Bredderman, T. (1983). "Effects of Activity-Based Elementary Science on Student Outcomes: A Quantitative Synthesis." *Review of Educational Research* 53, 4: 499–518.

Calderon, M., R. Hertz-Lazarowitz, and J. Tinajero. (1991). "Adapting CIRC to Multi-Ethnic and Bilingual Classrooms." *Cooperative Learning* 12, 1: 17–20.

Chamberlin, C., and E. Chamberlin. (1943). *Did They Succeed in College?* New York: Harper and Row.

Chesler, M., and R. Fox. (1966). *Role-Playing Methods in the Classroom.* Chicago: Science Research Associates, Inc.

Dewey, J. (1916). *Democracy in Education.* New York: Macmillan, Inc.

El-Nemr, M.A. (1979). "Meta-Analysis of the Outcomes of Teaching Biology as Inquiry." Unpublished doctoral diss., University of Colorado, Boulder.

Glass, G.V. (1982). "Meta-Analysis: An Approach to the Synthesis of Research Results." *Journal of Research in Science Teaching* 19, 2: 93–112.

Hertz-Lazarowitz, R. (1993). "Using Group Investigation to Enhance Arab-Jewish Relationships." *Cooperative Learning* 11, 2: 13–14.

Hillocks, G., Jr. (1987). "Synthesis of Research on Teaching Writing." *Educational Leadership* 44, 8: 71–82.

Johnson, D.W., and R.T. Johnson. (1981). "Effects of Cooperative and Individualistic Learning Experiences on Inter-Ethnic Interaction." *Journal of Educational Psychology* 73, 3: 444–449.

Johnson, D.W., and R.T. Johnson. (1989). *Cooperation and Competition: Theory and Research.* Edina, Minn.: Interaction Book Company.

Johnson, D.W., and R.T. Johnson. (1994). *Learning Together and Alone,* 13th ed. Englewood Cliffs, N.J.: Prentice-Hall.

Joyce, B., and E. Calhoun, eds. (1996). *Learning Experiences in School Renewal: An Exploration of Five Successful Programs.* Eugene, Oreg.: ERIC Clearinghouse.

Joyce, B., E. Calhoun, N. Carran, C. Halliburton, J. Simser, and D. Rust. (1994). "The Process and Effects of Three Governance Modes in Staff Development and School Renewal: A Field Study." Paper presented at the annual meeting of the Association for Supervision and Curriculum Development, Chicago.

Joyce, B., E. Calhoun, N. Carran, J. Simser, D. Rust, and C. Halliburton. (1996). "The University Town Program: Exploring Governance Structures." In *Learning Experiences in School Renewal*, edited by B. Joyce and E. Calhoun. Eugene, Oreg.: ERIC Clearinghouse.

Joyce, B., and B. Showers. (1983). *Power in Staff Development Through Research on Training.* Alexandria, Va.: Association for Supervision and Curriculum Development.

Joyce, B., B. Showers, and C. Rolheiser-Bennett. (1987). "Staff Development and Student Learning: A Synthesis of Research on Models of Teaching." *Educational Leadership* 45, 2: 11–23.

Joyce, B., and M. Weil. (1996). *Models of Teaching.* 5th ed. Boston: Allyn and Bacon.

Kagan, S. (1990). *Cooperative Learning Resources for Teachers.* San Juan Capistrano, Calif.: Resources for Teachers.

Neill, A.S. (1960). *Summerhill.* New York: Holt, Rinehart, and Winston.

Oakes, J. (1986). *Keeping Track: How Schools Structure Inequality.* New Haven, Conn.: Yale University Press.

Oliver, D., and J.P. Shaver. (1971). *Teaching Public Issues in the High School.* Boston: Houghton Mifflin.

Pinnell, G.S. (1989). "Helping At-Risk Children Learn to Read." *Elementary School Journal* 90, 2: 161–184.

Pressley, M., J.R. Levin, and H.D. Delaney. (1982). "The Mnemonic Keyword Method." *Review of Educational Research* 52, 1: 61–91.

Quellmalz, E.S., and J. Burry. (1983). *Analytic Scales for Assessing Students' Expository and Narrative Writing Skills.* (CSE Resource Paper No. 5). Los Angeles: Center for the Study of Evaluation, UCLA Graduate School of Education.

Roebuck, F., J. Buhler, and D. Aspy. (1976). "A Comparison of High and Low Levels of Humane Teaching/Learning Conditions on the Subsequent Achievement of Students Identified as Having Learning Difficulties." Final Report: Order No. PLD 6816–76 re. the National Institute of Mental Health. Denton, Tex.: Texas Woman's University Press.

Rogers, C. (1961). *On Becoming a Person.* Boston: Houghton Mifflin.

Rogers, C. (1982). *Freedom to Learn for the Eighties.* Columbus, Ohio: Charles E. Merrill.

Rolheiser-Bennett, C. (1986). *Four Models of Teaching: A Meta-Analysis of Student Outcomes.* Ph.D. Thesis, University of Oregon.

Shaftel, F., and G. Shaftel. (1982). *Role Playing in the Curriculum.* Englewood Cliffs, N.J.: Prentice-Hall.

Sharan, S., and H. Shachar. (1988). *Language and Learning in the Cooperative Classroom.* New York: Springer-Verlag.

Shaver, J.P. (1995). "Social Studies." In *Handbook of Research on Improving Instruction,* edited by G. Caweelti. Arlington, Va.: Alliance for Curriculum Reform.

Showers, B., B. Joyce, and B. Bennett. (1987). "Synthesis of Research on Staff Development: A Framework for Future Study and a State-of-the-Art Analysis." *Educational Leadership* 45, 3: 77–87.

Skinner, B.F. (1953). *Science and Human Behavior.* New York: Macmillan, Inc.

Slavin, R.E. (1983). *Cooperative Learning.* New York: Longman, Inc.

Slavin, R.E., and N.A. Madden. (1995). "Success for All: Creating Schools and Classrooms Where All Children Can Read." In *Creating New Educational Communities. The Ninety-Fourth Yearbook of the National Society for the Study of Education,* edited by J. Oakes and K. Quartz. Chicago: University of Chicago Press.

Smith, K., and M. Smith. (1966). *Cybernetic Principles of Learning and Educational Design.* New York: Holt, Rinehart, and Winston.

Smith, M.L. (1980). "Effects of Aesthetics Educations on Basic Skills Learning." Boulder: Laboratory of Educational Research, University of Colorado.

Spaulding, R. (1970). *E.I.P.* Durham, N.C.: Duke University Press.

Taba, H. (1966). *Teaching Strategies and Cognitive Functioning in Elementary School Children.* (Cooperative Research Project 2404). San Francisco: San Francisco State College.

Thelen, H. (1960). *Education and the Human Quest.* New York: Harper and Row.

Thoresen, C.E., and M.J. Mahoney. (1974). *Behavioral Self-Control.* New York: Holt, Rinehart, and Winston.

White, S.H. (1978). *Teaching and Learning.* Washington, D.C.: National Institute of Education.

Wolpe, J., and A. Lazarus. (1966). *Behavior Therapy Techniques: A Guide to the Treatment of Neuroses.* Oxford: Pergamon Press, Inc.

Bibliography

Aspy, D.N., F. Roebuck, M. Willson, and O. Adams. (1974). *Interpersonal Skills Training for Teachers.* (Interim report #2 for NIMH Grant #5PO 1MH 19871). Monroe: Northeast Louisiana University.

Ausubel, D.P. (1960). "The Use of Advance Organizers in the Learning and Retention of Meaningful Verbal Material." *Journal of Educational Psychology* 51, 4: 267–272.

Ausubel, D.P. (1963). *The Psychology of Meaningful Verbal Learning.* New York: Grune and Stratton, Inc.

Ausubel, D.P. (1968). *Educational Psychology: A Cognitive View.* New York: Holt, Rinehart, and Winston.

Ausubel, D.P. (1977). *Behavior Modification for the Classroom Teacher.* New York: McGraw-Hill.

Ausubel, D.P. (1980). "Schemata, Cognitive Structure, and Advance Organizers: A Reply to Anderson, Spiro, and Anderson." *American Educational Research Journal* 17, 3: 400–404.

Ausubel, D.P., and J. Fitzgerald. (1962). "Organizer, General Background and Antecedent Learning Variables in Sequential Verbal Learning." *Journal of Educational Psychology* 53, 2: 243–249.

Ausubel, D.P., M. Stager, and A.J.H. Gaite. (1968). "Retroactive Facilitation of Meaningful Verbal Learning." *Journal of Educational Psychology* 59, 3: 250–255.

Bonstingl, J.J. (1992). *Schools of Quality: An Introduction to Total Quality Management in Education.* Alexandria, Va.: Association for Supervision and Curriculum Development.

Brophy, J. E., and T. Good. (1986). "Teacher Behavior and Student Achievement." In *Handbook of Research on Teaching*, 3rd ed., edited by M. Wittrock. New York: Macmillan Publishing Co.

Bruner, J., J.J. Goodnow, and G.A. Austin. (1967). *A Study of Thinking.* New York: Science Editions, Inc.

Glasser, W. (1969). *Schools Without Failure.* New York: Harper and Row.

Good, T., D. Grouws, and H. Ebmeier. (1983). *Active Mathematics Teaching.* New York: Longman, Inc.

Hunt, D.E., L.F. Butler, J.E. Noy, and M.E. Rosser. (1978). *Assessing Conceptual Level by The Paragraph Completion Method.* Toronto: Ontario Institute for Studies in Education.

Hunt, D.E., J. Greenwood, R. Brill, and M. Deineka. (1972). "From Psychological Theory to Educational Practice: Implementation of a Matching Model." Symposium presented at the annual meeting of the American Educational Research Association, Chicago.

Hunt, D.E., and R.H. Hardt. (1967). "The Role of Conceptual Level and Program Structure in Summer Upward Bound Programs." Paper presented to the Eastern Psychological Association, Boston.

Hunt, D.E., and B. Joyce. (1967). "Teacher Trainee Personality and Initial Teaching Style." *American Educational Research Journal* 4, 1: 253–259.

Hunt, D.E., B. Joyce, and J. Del Popolo. (1964). "An Exploratory Study of the Modification of Student Teachers' Behavior Patterns." Unpublished paper, Syracuse University.

Hunt, D.E., B. Joyce, J. Greenwood, J. Noy, R. Reid, and M. Weil. (1981). Student Conceptual Level and Models of Teaching. In *Flexibility in Teaching,* edited by B. Joyce, L. Peck, and C. Brown. White Plains, N.Y.: Longman, Inc.

Hunt, D.E., and E.V. Sullivan. (1974). *Between Psychology and Education.* Hinsdale, Ill.: Dryden.

Johnson, D.W., and R.T. Johnson. (1974). "Instructional Goal Structure: Cooperative, Competitive, or Individualistic." *Review of Educational Research* 44, 2: 213–240.

Johnson, D.W., and R.T. Johnson. (1979). "Conflict in the Classroom: Controversy in Learning." *Review of Educational Research* 49, 1: 51–70.

Johnson, D.W., G. Maruyama, R. Johnson, D. Nelson, and L. Skon. (1981). "Effects of Cooperative, Competitive, and Individualistic Goal Structures on Achievement: A Meta-Analysis." *Psychological Bulletin* 89, 1: 47–62.

Joyce, B., and B. Showers. (1995). *Student Achievement Through Staff Development*. White Plains: Longman, Inc..

Maslow, A. (1962). *Toward a Psychology of Being*. New York: Van Nostrand.

Massialas, B., and B. Cox. (1966). *Inquiry in Social Studies*. New York: McGraw-Hill.

McKibbin, M., B. Joyce, and R.H. Hersh. (1983). *The Structure of School Improvement*. New York: Longman, Inc.

Nelson, J. (1971). "Collegial Supervision in Multi-Unit Schools." Ph.D. Thesis, University of Oregon.

Perls, F. (1968). *Gestalt Therapy Verbatim*. Lafayette, Calif.: Real People Press.

Rogers, C. (1969). *Freedom to Learn*. Columbus, Ohio: Charles E. Merrill.

Rogers, C. (1971). *Client-Centered Therapy*. Boston: Houghton Mifflin.

Rogers, C. (1981). *A Way of Being*. Boston: Houghton Mifflin.

Schwab, J. (1965). *Biological Sciences Curriculum Study: Biology Teachers' Handbook*. New York: John Wiley and Sons, Inc.

Schwab, J. (1982). *Science, Curriculum, and Liberal Education: Selected Essays*. Chicago: University of Chicago Press.

Schwab, J., and P. Brandwein. (1962). *The Teaching of Science*. Cambridge, Mass.: Harvard University Press.

Sharan, S., ed. (1994). *Handbook of Cooperative Learning Methods*. Westport, Conn.: Greenwood Press.

Sharan, Y., and S. Sharan. (1992). *Expanding Cooperative Learning Through Group Investigation*. New York: Teachers College Press.

Sigel, I.E. (1984). *Advances in Applied Developmental Psychology*. New York: Ablex.

Skinner, B.F. (1968). *The Technology of Teaching*. Englewood Cliffs, N.J.: Prentice-Hall.

Skinner, B.F. (1971). *Beyond Freedom and Dignity*. New York: Knopf.

Suchman, R.J. (1981). *Idea Book for Geological Inquiry*. New York: Trillium Press.

White, W.A.T. (1986). "The Effects of Direct Instruction in Special Education: A Meta-Analysis." Ph.D. Thesis, University of Oregon.

Worthen, B. (1968). "A Study of Discovery and Expository Presentation: Implications for Teaching." *Journal of Teacher Education* 19, 2: 223–242.